NEW PUBLIC MANAGEMENT

About the Authors

Ganapathy Palanithurai, Professor in Rajiv Gandhi Chair, Gandhigram Rural Institute is an academic activist working with the people in rural areas for building the capacity of the leaders and people to reinvent sustainable grassroots democracy. He is heading the Department of Political Science and Development Administration, in Gandhigram Rural University, Tamil Nadu. His policy advocacy role at the governmental level is increasingly felt at present in all the three levels, namely, sub-regional, regional and national as he does more field work than theorization. He has been associating himself with State Planning Commission of Tamil Nadu, Population Foundation of India, Rajiv Gandhi Foundation, CAPART, Ministry of Rural Areas and Employment and DANIDA (Danish-Indo Development Agency) in specific areas of activities in connection with empowerment of people. He is in the network of the Non-Governmental Organisations for Panchayat activities. He involves himself in capacity building exercise for local body leaders. He has evolved training module and manual for local body leaders. He has to his credit twenty-four books, seventy-five articles in reputed journals, ten working papers, seven monographs, seven review articles on three major areas, namely, Legislative Behaviour, Ethnicity and Panchayati Raj System. He was a recipient of Fellowship from Sastri Indo-Canadian Institute, New Delhi and World Academy of Art and Science, USA. He has visited the US and Canada, on academic assignments. He was a visiting fellow in the MiGill University, Canada in 1989. He is a life member of Indian Institute of Public Administration, Indian Association of Public Administration, Indian Association of Political Science, Indian Association of American Studies, and Indian Association of Canadian Studies. He is a member of the expert committee constituted by the Government of Tamil Nadu, to monitor the training programme for local body leaders.

Vanishree Joseph is a Research Fellow, pursuing her research programme in "Gender and Governance". She has been involving in organizing Panchayat women leaders for social development activities. She has received awards for her contribution in the forms of articles and presentations in the areas of gender and governance based on her field activities. She has written a few monographs on the same area. She is in a network of scholars working in the field of Capability Approach.

Sivakumar Somasundaram is a Research Fellow, working for his research programme on Women Empowerment. He is an active field worker.

NEW PUBLIC MANAGEMENT

(A Case Analysis of District Administration)

G. Palanithurai
J. Vanishree
S. Sivakumar

CONCEPT PUBLISHING COMPANY, NEW DELHI-110059

Cataloging in Publication Data—DK *New Public Management*
Courtesy: D.K. Agencies (P) Ltd. <docinfo@dkagencies.com>

Palanithurai, G. (Ganapathy), 1953-
New public management : a case analysis of district administration / G. Palanithurai, J.Vanishree, S. Sivakumar.
p. cm.
Study conducted at Pudukkottai District of Tamil Nadu, India.
Includes bibliographical references (p.)
Includes index.
ISBN 8180692620

1. Rural development projects—India—Pudukkottai (District)—Citizen participation. 2. Pudukkottai (India : District)—Politics and government. I. Vanishree, J. (Joseph), joint author. II. Sivakumar, S. (Somasundaram), joint author. III. Title.

DDC 307.141 209 548 2 21

ISBN : 81-8069-262-0

First Published 2006

Published and Printed by
Ashok Kumar Mittal
Concept Publishing Company
A/15-16, Commercial Block, Mohan Garden,
New Delhi-110059 (India)
Phones : 25351460, 25351794
Fax : +91-11-25357103
Email : publishing@conceptpub.com

PREFACE

The twenty first century is marked for increasing demand for services by the people, high political awareness, high level of public intolerance, dwindling faith in government machinery, expediency in public life, high proficiency in technical skills, professionalism in all work, increasing speed of human activities through developed communication systems and high exploitation of natural resources, which have prompted the State and the Central Governments to look for an alternative and efficient delivery system which will deliver the goods to the public with a sense of commitment. This requires new attitude and behaviour on the part of the personnel who are at the helm of affairs in institutions. As a result two new areas have emerged in Public Administration, namely, New Public Management and New Development Administration. New Public Management and New Development Administration are conceptually and operationally sound in the developed countries which have been geared up for this new course both by the policy makers and administrators and by the people. But in many of the developing countries this has been introduced as a part of the reform package in consonance with the globalization of the economy. While looking at the ramifications one can see contradictions and problems as the level of understanding of the framework is low. In India it is a subject for academic discussion and, when it comes to practice, one can find this in practice only very rarely.

The present writeup is the result of a curious analysis of the role of the District Administration under the supervision and direction of the District Collector in the development process. When some of the activities of the District Collector of Pudukkottai District were reported in newspapers, we started looking at the activities of the Collector in the development schemes meant for the poor. As we found interesting developments in the District Administration in the context of reform, we have undertaken a study and evaluated some of the schemes implemented for the rural poor. The whole study has been carried out against the backdrop of the principles of the New Public Management.

To complete this work, a number of people have helped us to collect the needed data and confirm the same. Officials at the block level extended their fullest cooperation and they also gave their views and opinions on the schemes when the research team interacted with them. Development participants (beneficiaries) of the schemes helped the research team by providing needed information. After the evaluation and analysis the District Collector and the Project Officer DRDA were requested to interact with the team on the points which emerged from the evaluation. Both have frankly expressed their opinions on each and every item.

We sincerely express our deep sense of gratitude to the District Collector Thiru.Hitesh Kumar S.Makwana, the Project Officer, DRDA, Thiru.S.Selvaraj, officials working at Block level in the district of Pudukkottai and the development participants (beneficiaries) for their generosity in sparing their valuable time for us and for providing necessary inputs for this exercise. We thank our colleagues working in the Rajiv Gandhi Chair for Panchayati Raj Studies and The Hunger Project for their constant support to this task. We express our sincere gratitude to the authorities of the Institute for providing an opportunity to undertake this study in Pudukkottai District.

G. Palanithurai
J. Vanishree
S. Sivakumar

CONTENTS

LIST OF TABLES

LIST OF ABBREVIATIONS

APO	Assistant Project Officer
BDO	Block Development Officer
BPL	Below Poverty Line
BT Road	Black Top Road
CAG	Comptroller and Auditor General
CC	Cement Concrete
CCS	Credit-cum-Subsidy Scheme
CWP	Comprehensive Water Programme
DPAP	Drought Prone Area Programme
DRDA	District Rural Development Agency
DSMS	District Supply and Marketing Society
DWACRA	Development of Women and Children in Rural Areas
EAS	Employment Assurance Scheme
FAQ	Fair Average Quantity
FCI	Food Corporation of India
GC	Governing Council
GH	Government Hospital
IAY	Indira Awaas Yojana
IEC	Information Education Campaign
ISCWC	Integrated Sanitary Complex for Women and Children
IWDP	Integrated Wasteland Development Programme
JGSY	Jawahar Gram Samridhi Yojana
JRY	Jawahar Rozgar Yojana
KVIC	Khadi & Village Industries Commission
MI Tank	Minor Irrigation Tank
MS	Mukkiya Sevika
MT	Mahalir Thittam

NGO	Non Governmental Organization
PDS	Public Distribution System
PH	Physically Handicapped
PO	Project Officer
PRI	Panchayati Raj Institution
RCC	Reinforced Cement Concrete
RCH	Reproductive & Child Health
RD	Rural Development
RLEGP	Rural Landless Employment Guarantee Programme
SC	Scheduled Caste
SGSY	Swarnajayanthi Gram Swarozgar Yojana
SHG	Self Help Group
ST	Scheduled Tribe
STAMIN	State Agricultural Extension Management Training Institute
TRSP	Total Rural Sanitation Programme
UG	User Group
UNICEF	United Nations International Children and Educational Fund
UT	Union Territory
WSC	Women's Sanitary Complex
ZP	Zilla Parishad

1

INTRODUCTION

The twenty-first century is marked for high degree of awareness among the people, high people's expectations, high public intolerance, increasing resourcefulness of individuals who are involved in the management of institutions and organizations, flexible and adaptable structures, and, simplified procedures in public administration and in the conduct of state governments and the bureaucracy.

For any transformation and development people are the *sine quo non* and they are the factors determining the nature and the quantum of change and development. How we look at people matters much in the development process. What is more important is that how people look at themselves in society and how they perceive themselves in the development process determine the course of development. The whole process of development revolves round the human being and other factors like capital and technology, which constitute imperatives, but are secondary in nature, while people are considered primary. The next question is how people are used or how they use themselves in the development process. In the present context state initiatives are dormant in many of the developing countries of the world. In India the culture of state initiated development activities has taken strong root in the minds of the people. But now a paradigm shift is visible in the development process. The present writeup will throw light on people's involvement in the development process against the backdrop of the facilitation by the state of the new paradigm.

The Indian Independence movement demonstrated to the world that the human energy unleashed by the Indian masses through the channels formed by the leaders is capable of bringing about needed social and economic transformation provided they are properly motivated. But, at the dawn of independence, a strong feeling and perception arose among the elites that modernization, westernization and industrialization could bring about needed development in the economy of this country. This dominant thought percolated into the minds of the elites and thereby they developed the idea that the economy of this country and social transformation could be achieved by scientific planning at the top and that the same could be implemented by the bureaucracy very effectively. In the whole process the ruling elites undermined the potential of the human energy and the people participated in implementation of only the development activities initiated by the government. Slowly and steadily the bureaucracy expanded its structure and usurped the powers of the community.

There was a logical argument for the expansion of the bureaucratic machinery as people did not come up to the level of expectation in implementing the development programmes and schemes owing to the reason that the people took time to perceive the programmes properly and implement the same effectively but the bureaucracy took a shorter time to understand and implement the programmes. Further, the government posited to itself that it could make the people accept whatever it did. But people cannot do what the government does as the people are the community and unless the people accept no programme can be implemented by the people collectively. By continuously following this style people were driven away from the realm of governance and thereby a perceptible gap was created between the people and the government.

Within a short period of time the government machinery developed into a leviathan and acquired the character of a dictator. Government offices and officers have virtually taken over the development activities. They plan for the development of the people continuously through the planning exercises and yet they cannot achieve anything substantial in reducing poverty and providing minimum basic facilities to the people to lead a dignified decent human life in society. The Government, by its muscle, has proliferated schemes and programmes and millions of rupees have been spent and yet the basic demands of the poverty stricken cannot be met.

But there are a few sections in Indian society who, through the party system, have understood the whole process of governance and appropriately colluded with the bureaucracy and ensured a system of governance for their own advantage. People in society believe that the government and its machinery are always powerful and do justice and that they can expect benefits and justice from the government. That is the reason why the government survives and people obey its procedures and rules. The proliferation of rules and procedures in administration gives room for exploitation as people can not monitor the administration. There is yet another phenomenon which attracts the attention of all. Though India got Independence from the British the people could not get independence from the British administration as free India continued the British type of administration.

As it was convenient to the ruling elites they wanted to continue the British administrative system with adaptations. Indian administrative thinkers could not suggest an indigenous system of administration to replace the system established by the British. Though we hail the administrative ethos in ancient Indian society we cannot evolve a viable vibrant alternative administrative system which requires enormous energy on the part of the administrative thinkers. In the absence of an indigenous system this kind of administrative arrangement helped the politicians and bureaucrats to gain perfect understanding about the whole process of governance and development and to keep the people away from the process of governance and development. Despite the efforts of the government in administering development and providing services discontent grew in society over the neglect of the rustic people in the development process. Social conflict is intensive, corruption is rampant, the state is weakened and the government has lost its credibility in the eyes of the people. Yet the government functions and performs its role and responsibility not with comfort but with much difficulty. The above said conditions prompted the introduction of several changes in public administration.

In recent decades the growing crisis in administration and the changes in the global environment have tended to redefine the role of the government and its functions. To ensure efficiency, economy and effectiveness changes have been made in the administrative system to cope with the emerging challenges of society. The new approach to the administration focuses on empowering and enabling community organizations to solve their own problems, a shift in the working pattern from hierarchy to participation and team work, meeting and working towards customers and not the bureaucracy, and, emphasis on earning and resource mobilization rather than on spending. In addition, transformation from rule-driven government into mission oriented government has brought about some changes in government policies on development and the administration has been geared towards meeting human needs. Previously the multiplicity of Rural Development programmes implemented in the course of five decades were viewed as separate programmes, which resulted in a lack of proper social intermediation and failed to realize the inherent capabilities of the people. The procedure oriented bureaucracy complicated the process further and failed to deliver the desirable results. The failure in the implementation of these development programmes pointed to the critical role of the ordinary citizen in ensuring the success of development initiatives.

But at present governance has become an affair of many, not only the affair of the government. It needs more partners, new principles, a new framework, new values and new norms. Government institutions have failed and as a result they have been removed from the centre stage and people's organizations are coming to the forefront to take up new responsibilities. Thus governance at present needs a shared vision to bring about development and administer social justice and equity. In the new dispensation development activities have to be evaluated at every level and at every stage for midcourse correction.

In India people's participation is only a slogan and not a principle to be practised. To make the people participate in the process of development the political system needs a political will. Indian society is highly politicized and hence one can see a high level of participation in politics but not in development activities. The greatest difficulty in the Indian setting is to recreate linkages between the people and the government. As the people have been driven out from the orbit of governance a wide gap has sprung up. To bring them back into the governing process as development participants new forms of participation have to be identified.

To bring the people closer to the Government the people's voice has to be strengthened. Their voice has to be cultured and properly shaped to focus on the issues of development. The concept of development has to be reconsidered in the context of crises in natural resource management, globalization of economy and its implications. Any development should follow the track of indigenous knowledge. People's knowledge can be utilized for development. There are many innovations in difficult fields and they are to be recognized. By recognizing innovations at the grassroots the citizens responsibility in the development process will be enhanced. A conducive climate is necessary for participatory governance. An alternative paradigm is needed for governance and development. Ultimately the changes suggested above can be effected only if the capacity of the policy makers and the bureaucrats is enhanced.

Citizens' participation offers a new way of thinking about development. It indicates that citizens can help themselves. They can articulate their own needs and find the means to fulfil them. They can be active participants rather than mere recipients of development benefits. Development works will bring about needed results if they are carried out in a demand driven mode. Through direct participation the people will be able to directly voice their needs and concerns and responsibilities. They can complement government initiatives with their own capability and thereby put their concerns before service providers to demand service outcomes. Since they are in the best position to articulate their needs and find appropriate means, to get better results through development programmes, "human needs centred development" is the need of the hour. Human needs-centered development revolves round the people and adopts flexible methods. Civil servants and the government assume greater responsibility for their actions and work in an unstructured format as development needs are dynamic and, as a result, different development methods are adopted. The administrative effectiveness will increase as the political leaders and the administrators will be service-minded and accountable to the public. Each and every individual will be treated with dignity and respect and recognized as an important member in society. The need is growing to focus on developmental efforts around the people.

One such effort was made in Pudukkottai District of Tamil Nadu by the district administration in implementing some of the rural development schemes of the Government of India. To achieve excellence in all areas and be a model the District Rural Development Agency, Pudukkottai, under the guidance of the District Collector, is trying to achieve maximum efficiency and efforts are being made to streamline programme implementation at all levels. To obtain maximum benefit from each programme various innovations are being tried along with the aim of achieving better results in all routine programmes.

Against this backdrop, this evaluation work has been carried out in Pudukkottai District with the help of the District Rural Development Agency from the academic perspective. The main purpose of this evaluation, is to critically review the development initiatives of the implementing agency with the participation of the people keeping in view the Indian situation. The role played by the so-called third stratum of government, i.e., Panchayati Raj Institutions (PRIs), is crucial in the ongoing process of development. These democratically decentralized institutions educate the people politically, serve as a training ground for political leadership, secure political stability through participation in formal politics, achieve political equality, enhance accountability and improve the responsiveness of the government. Further they give considerable promise of making the development projects more sustainable.

Theoretical Framework

The emergence of the new paradigm in public administration has added a new dimension to the whole of the political system and the manner in which power is exercised in utilizing the country's economic and social resources for development. Nowadays the phenomenon of governance has been changed into good governance. Good governance is associated with efficient and effective administration in a democratic framework. This is committed to improvement in the quality of life of the people and is equivalent to purposive and development oriented administration. It can be considered a citizen-friendly, citizen-caring and responsive administration. The operationalization of good governance can be carried out with a vital input called New Public Management. Recently significant changes have been taking place in managing public organizations, which aim at market based public administration resulting in effectiveness and economy in the functioning. This new perspective focuses on the cooperation and involvement of a large number of citizens and organizations. The role of the State in the New Public Management regime shrinks to that of a facilitator from that of a provider. Priorities, goals and strategies of development are completely reoriented and refocused in this approach. The State has metamorphosed from a Political State to an Administrative State and the Bureaucratic State is today on the threshold of becoming a Cybernetic State. The rationale behind the Political State was the creation of representative institutions through which power could be exercised and controlled. The transition to the Administrative State was due to the growth of industry, creation of new regulatory instruments and agencies in the 19th century and mobilization of administrative expertise to manage public activities. The Bureaucratic State came into being when the government role changed from regulation to operation. In the Cybernetic State, "government functions as a servo-mechanism, conjoining the polity and economy to achieve public objectives". The Cybernetic State envisages changes in government: new forms of community government to ensure greater participation and new structures for cybernetic guidance to keep the cybernetic process on track. All this transformation has been taking place to achieve excellence and optimum benefit to satisfy the human needs. The administration has to cope with the diversified needs of the people in the changing environment. Some of the well-known principles did not fulfil the desired expectations of society. The rigidity of the models did not suit the dynamic nature of society. Hence different approaches to suit the needs of society are emerging. This process, New Public Management, is the new perspective which has emerged as a new strategy to meet the needs of good governance. The prevailing environment demands institutions that are flexible and adaptable, that deliver high quality goods and services, that are responsive to their customers, that are led by persuasion and incentives rather than commands and that give their employees a sense of control, even ownership. Institutions need to empower citizens for tomorrow rather than simply serve them today. Keeping these aspects in mind, the New Public Management perspective was adopted to evaluate some of the development activities in the form of schemes in Pudukkottai District.

Objective of the Study

The main objective of the study is to ascertain the utility and success of government schemes with people's participation. In the era of globalization the state has started rethinking its role as a facilitator instead of as a provider. In this perspective the New Public Management strategy has been adopted in the execution of government activities. After independence a large number of welfare schemes and programmes were implemented to improve the status of rural India with more and more of Government intervention. But the achievements were not substantial. When we speak of social and political development, the involvement and participation of the people and of the government are inseparable. So far initiatives were taken by the government and programmes were carried out by the government with the involvement of the people. The participation of the people in this process was meagre and this may be one of the reasons for the failure of that government's schemes. To set right this state of affairs and move from inaction to action, people's participation has been initiated now. In order to find out this process of change this study has been undertaken in

Pudukkottai District to evaluate the innovative methods adopted in the implementation of government schemes with the participation of the stakeholders.

Schemes Evaluated

The New Public Management acquires special importance in the context of the ongoing process of globalization and associated economic reforms. This document attempts to articulate the connection between the economic dependence of vulnerable groups in the ongoing process and the role of the state in enabling the rural masses to come up from obscurity through several developmental programmes. There are umpteen number of programmes carried out for the upliftment of the rural poor in India. In order to be more specific, while assessing the outcomes, only a few schemes have been evaluated. These are:

(1) Indira Awaas Yojana

(2) Integrated Sanitary Complex for Women and Children

(3) Food for work under Sampoorna Grameen Rozgar Yojana (SGRY)

(4) District Supply and Marketing Society under Swarnajayanthi Gram Swarozgar Yojana (SGSY)

(5) Non Conventional Energy Sources – BIOGAS

Methodology

As mentioned earlier the present study aims at assessing the utility and the level of success of government schemes with people's participation. In order to make the study more objective only selected government schemes have been chosen for the evaluation. The implementation process of these selected schemes in all the 13 blocks of Pudukkottai District was evaluated. While choosing the study area, random sampling technique was adopted. Informal interview was conducted with the District Collector, Project Officer,

Mukkiya Sevikas and other social welfare workers, Village Panchayat Presidents and finally the beneficiaries to elicit their opinions about the government schemes and also to analyse the impact created by these schemes.

Indicators

The following indicators were adopted for evaluation in the present study:

-- To find out whether the scheme is implemented as per the government guidelines.
-- To find out if there is any qualitative change in the delivery system.
-- To find out the perception of the stakeholders about the schemes.
-- To measure the level of participation of the stakeholders in the schemes throughout the implementation process.
-- To analyse the role of the district administration in enhancing the participation level of the beneficiaries.
-- To identify the problems faced by the administration as well as the beneficiaries during the implementation and to study how these hurdles are tackled.
-- To find out if there is any contribution from the people, both in cash and in kind, towards the scheme.
-- To identify the ownership of the scheme (district administration or beneficiaries).
-- To identify the intervention intensity (whether the scheme is felt to be needed by the people or it is a supply based work of the administration).
-- To identify the role of the district administration as a facilitator.
-- To identify the innovative practices.
-- To analyse the causes for the success.
-- To analyse the level of utility of the scheme.

Structure of the Report

The present report has six chapters including the introduction and the conclusion. The second chapter presents the evaluative report of the research team on the schemes. The third chapter provides insights into the perception of the District Collector of the issues of development and the involvement of the people and the bureaucracy. The fourth chapter deals with the outlook of the Project Officer DRDA on the process of development and the participation of people and bureaucracy in the development activities at the grassroots. The fifth chapter presents the overall evaluation of the schemes.

2

EVALUATION OF SCHEMES

INDIRA AWAAS YOJANA

The Indira Awaas Yojana (IAY) was launched during 1985-86 as a sub-scheme of the Rural Landless Employment Guarantee Programme (RLEGP) and continued as a sub-scheme of the Jawahar Rozgar Yojana (JRY) since its launching in April 1989. It has been delinked from the JRY and has been made an independent scheme with effect from 1st January, 1996. The objective of the IAY is primarily to provide grants for construction of houses to members of the Scheduled Castes/Scheduled Tribes, non-SC/ST rural poor people below the poverty line and freed bonded labourers. The target group for houses under the IAY will be people below the poverty line living in rural areas belonging to Scheduled Castes/Scheduled Tribes and non-SC/ST communities and freed bonded labourers subject to the condition that the benefits to the non-SC/ST communities should not exceed 40 per cent of the total IAY allocation during a financial year. From 1995-96 the IAY benefits have been extended to ex-servicemen, widows or the next-of-kin of defence personnel and personnel of paramilitary forces killed in action, irrespective of the income criteria on subject to the condition that :

(i) they reside in rural areas;
(ii) they have not been covered under any other scheme of shelter rehabilitation; and
(iii) they are houseless or in need of shelter or shelter upgradation.

Priority is to be given to ex-servicemen and retired members of the paramilitary forces as long as they fulfil the normal eligibility conditions of the IAY and have not been covered under any other shelter rehabilitation scheme. The priority in the matter of allotment of houses to the ex-servicemen and paramilitary personnel and their dependents will be out of the 40 per cent of the houses set apart for allotment to the non-SC/ST categories of beneficiaries with 3 per cent of the funds being earmarked for the benefit of disabled persons below the poverty line. This reservation of 3 per cent under the IAY for disabled persons below the poverty line will be a horizontal reservation, i.e., disabled persons belonging to sections like SCs, STs and others will be accommodated in their respective categories.

Identification of Beneficiaries

The District/Zilla Parishad Rural Development Agency (DRDA), on the basis of the allocation made and the targets fixed, shall decide Panchayatwise number of houses to be constructed under the IAY during a particular financial year and intimate the same to the Gram Panchayat. Thereafter the Gram Sabha will select the beneficiaries, restricting the number to the target allotted from the list of eligible households, according to the IAY guidelines and as per the priorities fixed. No approval of the Panchayat Samiti/Council will be required. The Panchayat Samiti/Council should however, be sent a list of the selected beneficiaries for information. The order of priority for selection of beneficiaries among the target group below the poverty line is as follows:

(i) Freed bonded labourers,

(ii) SC/ST households who are victims of atrocities,

(iii) SC/ST households headed by widows and unmarried women,

(iv) SC/ST households affected by flood, fire, earthquake, cyclone and similar natural calamities,

(v) Other SC/ST households,

(vi) Non-SC/ST households,

(vii) Physically handicapped,

(viii) Families/widows of personnel of defence services/ paramilitary forces killed in action, and

(ix) Displaced persons on account of developmental projects, nomadic, semi-nomadic, and de-notified tribals, families with disabled members and internal refugees, subject to the households being below the poverty line.

Allotment of houses should be in the name of the females of the beneficiary households. Alternatively, they can be allotted in the name of both husband and wife.

Pattern of Funding

The IAY is a centrally sponsored scheme funded on cost sharing basis between the Government of India and the States in the ratio of 80:20. In the case of Union Territories, the entire resources under this scheme are provided by the Government of India. Central assistance under the IAY will be allocated to the States/UTs on the basis of proportion of rural poor in a State/UT to the total poor in the country. The poverty estimate prepared by the Planning Commission in this regard will be used for this purpose. The proportion of rural SC/ST population in a district to the total rural SC/ST population in the State/UT is the criterion of inter-district allocation of IAY funds by the State/UT. The allocation for every year will be determined by the Government of India on the basis of the above criteria subject to availability of funds. At present the upper limit of construction assistance under the IAY is as given in Table 2.1

Table 2.1 : Upper Limit of Construction Assistance under IAY

	Plain Areas			Hilly/Difficult Areas		
	Central Govt. Rs.	State Govt. Rs.	Total Rs.	Central Govt Rs.	State Govt Rs.	Total Rs.
Construction of house including sanitary latrine and smokeless chuha	13,125	4,375	17,500	14,625	4,875	19,500
Cost of providing infrastructure and common facilities	1,875	625	2,500	1,875	625	2,500
Grant from State Government for concrete roof	—	12,000	12,000	—	12,000	12,000
Total	15,000	17,000	32,000	16,500	17,500	34,000

Source: IAY Guidelines

Involvement of Beneficiaries

As per the IAY guidelines the construction of the houses should be done by the beneficiaries themselves from the very beginning. The beneficiaries may make their own arrangements for the construction, engage skilled workmen on their own and also contribute family labour. The beneficiaries will have complete freedom as to the manner of construction of the house which is their own. This will result in economy in cost, ensure quality of construction, lead to satisfaction on the part of the beneficiaries and acceptance of the house. The responsibility for the proper construction of the house will thus be on the beneficiaries themselves. No contactor is allowed in the construction of IAY houses. The house should not also be constructed by any Government department. Government departments or organizations can, however, give technical assistance or arrange for coordinated supply of raw materials such as cement, steel or bricks if the beneficiaries so decide. The spirit of the IAY is that the house is not to be constructed and delivered by any external agency; on the other hand, the house is to be constructed by the ultimate occupier of the house. The guidelines also state that while fixing the technical specifications efforts should be made to utilize to the maximum possible extent local materials and cost effective technologies developed by various institutions. No type of design is to be imposed on the beneficiary as per the guidelines. The layout, the size and design type of IAY houses should depend on the local conditions. Hence, no design type is prescribed for IAY houses except that the plinth area of the houses should be around 20 sq. mts. The houses should be designed in accordance with the desire of the beneficiaries, keeping in view the climatic conditions and the need to provide proper space, kitchen, ventilation, sanitary facilities, smokeless chulha, etc. The Ministry of Non-Conventional Energy Sources encourages installation of fuel efficient chulhas. The guidelines also ensure that every house constructed under the IAY is provided with a fuel efficient chulha.

In tune with these guidelines, Pudukkottai District of Tamil Nadu carried out the IAY programme broadly going by the flexibility provisions incorporated. The DRDA, Pudukkottai, has successfully tried innovations in design, building materials, construction and labour use in the district.

Quantum of Work Done

IAY houses were constructed in all the thirteen blocks of Pudukkottai District. The blockwise details of the allocation of IAY houses in 2002-2003 are given in the following pages (Tables 2.2to 2.15):

Table 2.2 : Blockwise details of the allocation of IAY houses in 2002-2003 in Pudukkottai District

Sl. No.	Name of the Block	Total No. of houses sanctioned
1.	Annavasal	197
2.	Arimalam	109
3.	Kunnandarkoil	117
4.	Ponnamaravathi	107
5.	Pudukkottai	100
6.	Thirumayam	129
7.	Viralimalai	164
8.	Aranthangi	157
9.	Avudayarkoil	106
10.	Gandarvakottai	203
11.	Karambakudi	143
12.	Manamelkudi	79
13.	Thiruvarankuam	170
	Total	**1781**

Source: Records, DRDA, Pudukkottai District.

Table 2.3 : Village Panchayatwise details of the allocation of IAY houses of Annavasal Union 2002-2003

Sl. No.	Name of the Village Panchayat	Total No. of houses sanctioned
1.	Chitannavasal	10
2.	Edayapatti	20
3.	Keelakurichi	19
4.	Kilikudi	1
5.	Kudimiyanmalai	20
6.	Mangudi	15
7.	Mathiyanallur	14
8.	Melur	5
9.	Mukkanamalaipatti	9
10.	Narthamalai	10
11.	Panampatti	5
12.	Parambur	5
13.	Perumanadu	10
14.	Pudur	10
15.	Rapoosal	1
16.	Thiruvengaivasal	20
17.	Vayalogam	6
18.	Veerapatti	7
19.	Vellanur	10
	Total	**197**

Source: Records, DRDA, Pudukkottai District.

Table 2.4 : Village Panchayatwise details of the allocation of IAY houses of Arimalam Union 2002-2003

Sl. No.	Name of the Village Panchayat	Total No. of houses sanctioned
1.	K.Chettipatti	20
2.	Kadayakudi	1
3.	Kadiyapatti	10
4.	Kannangarakudi	7
5.	Kummangudi	1
6.	Medhagam	8
7.	Melnilaivayal	5
8.	Nallammalsamudram	9
9.	Onangudi	15
10.	Pdunilaivayal	4
11.	Samudram	7
12.	Thiruvakudi	17
13.	Valaramanickam	5
	Total	**109**

Source: Records, DRDA, Pudukkottai District.

Table 2.5 : Village Panchayatwise details of the allocation of IAY houses of Thirumayam Union 2002-2003

Sl. No.	Name of the Village Panchayat	Total No. of houses sanctioned
1.	Adhanur	10
2.	Aranginampatti	20
3.	Elanjavur	10
4.	Kottaiyur	10
5.	Kulamangalam	10
6.	Kutipirai	10
7.	Melur	10
8.	Oonaiyur	14
9.	Peraiyur	20
10.	Pilivalam	5
11.	Thirumayam	10
	Total	**129**

Source: Records, DRDA, Pudukkottai District.

Table 2.6 : Village Panchayatwise details of the allocation of IAY houses of Pudukkottai Union 2002-2003

Sl. No.	Name of the Village Panchayat	Total No. of houses sanctioned
1.	Manglathupatti	10
2.	Mookampatti	27
3.	Pudukkottai	37
4.	Puthambur	20
5.	Vadvalam	5
6.	Valavampatti	11
	Total	**100**

Source: Records, DRDA, Pudukkottai District.

Table 2.7 : Village Panchayatwise details of the allocation of IAY houses of Ponnamaravathi Union 2002-2003

Sl. No.	Name of the Village Panchayat	Total No. of houses sanctioned
1.	Ammakurichi	10
2.	Arasamalai	8
3.	Kallampatty	1
4.	Kandiyanatham	10
5.	Mullipatti	8
6.	Nallur	8
7.	Maravamadurai	20
8.	Semboothi	15
9.	Sevalur	9
10.	Thenur	10
11.	Varpattu	8
	Total	**107**

Source: Records, DRDA, Pudukkottai District.

Table 2.8 : Village Panchayatwise details of the allocation of IAY houses of Kunnandarkoil Union 2002-2003

Sl. No.	Name of the Village Panchayat	Total No. of houses sanctioned
1.	Killanur	18
2.	Killukulavaipatti	10
3.	Kulathur	3
4.	Melpuduvayal	1
5.	Nanjur	10
6.	Odurkkur	2
7.	Pallathupatti	8
8.	Perambur	10
9.	Puliyur	6
10.	Themmavur	12
11.	Vaithur	9
12.	Valamangalam	10
13.	Valiyampatti	10
14.	Vathnakottai	8
	Total	**117**

Source: Records, DRDA, Pudukkottai District.

Table 2.9 : Village Panchayatwise details of the allocation of IAY houses of Viralimalai Union 2002-2003

Sl. No.	Name of the Village Panchayat	Total No. of houses sanctioned
1.	Agarapatti	15
2.	Alangudi	1
3.	Avoor	12
4.	Kalamarur	1
5.	Kathalur	10
6.	Kunnathur	7
7.	Madhyanipatti	10
8.	Meenaveli	5
9.	Nadupatti	6
10.	Nambampatti	10
11.	Palandampatti	5
12.	Rajalipatti	10
13.	Thengaithinnipatti	10
14.	Venathirayanpatti	10
15.	Vilapatti	5
16.	Vemmani	5
17.	Viralimalai	32
18.	Virudhapatti	10
	Total	**164**

Source: Records, DRDA, Pudukkottai District.

Table 2.10 : Village Panchayatwise details of the allocation of IAY houses of Aranthangi Union 2002-2003

Sl. No.	Name of the Village Panchayat	Total No. of houses sanctioned
1.	Avanathankottai	5
2.	Eaiyur	20
3.	Kammangadu	7
4.	Keelkudiammanjakki	7
5.	Melapattu	20
6.	Nagudi	22
7.	Nattumangalam	10
8.	Oorvani	10
9.	Panchatti	10
10.	Perungadu	5
11.	Poovathakudi	10
12.	Rajendrapuram	10
13.	Thanthani	5
14.	Vallvari	11
15.	Vembangudi East	5
	Total	**157**

Source: Records, DRDA, Pudukkottai District.

Table 2.11 : Village Panchayatwise details of the allocation of IAY houses of Avudayarkoil Union 2002-2003

Sl. No.	Name of the Village Panchayat	Total No. of houses sanctioned
1.	Keelacheri	20
2.	Kundagavayal	12
3.	Perunavalur	10
4.	Poovalur	9
5.	Puthambur	5
6.	Senganam	10
7.	Sirumaruthur	20
8.	Thunjanur	10
9.	Vilanur	10
	Total	**106**

Source: Records, DRDA, Pudukkottai District.

Table 2.12 : Village Panchayatwise details of the allocation of IAY houses of Manamelkudi Union 2002-2003

Sl. No.	Name of the Village Panchayat	Total No. of houses sanctioned
1.	Bramanavayal	5
2.	Kanadu	7
3.	Kattumavadi	3
4.	Kolendram	10
5.	Manalur	17
6.	Minnamozhi	3
7.	Nelveli	10
8.	Sathiyadi	10
9.	Thandalai	9
10.	Vellur	5
	Total	**79**

Source: Records, DRDA, Pudukkottai District.

Table 2.13 : Village Panchayatwise details of the allocation of IAY houses of Karambakudi Union 2002-2003

Sl. No.	Name of the Village Panchayat	Total No. of houses sanctioned
1.	Elagaviduthi	18
2.	Kanakkankadu	15
3.	Keerathur	12
4.	Malaiyur	5
5.	Mullankurichi	23
6.	Pilaviduthi	15
7.	Pudhuviduthi	10
8.	Ponnanviduthi	20
9.	Karukeeltheru	10
10.	Rangianviduthi	15
	Total	**143**

Source: Records, DRDA, Pudukkottai District.

Table 2.14 : Village Panchayatwise details of the allocation of IAY houses of Gandarvakottai Union 2002-2003

Sl. No.	Name of the Village Panchayat	Total No. of houses sanctioned
1.	Akkachipatti	19
2.	Andanur	10
3.	Gomapuram	10
4.	Kattunaval	20
5.	Kulathur	20
6.	Manjapettai	10
7.	Nadupatti	10
8.	Namburanpatti	9
9.	Nathamadipatti	1
10.	Palaya Gandarvakottai	15
11.	Periyakottai	20
12.	Pisanathur	10
13.	Pudunagar	4
14.	Pudupatti	8
15.	Thurusupatti	22
16.	Thuvar	2
17.	Vadugapatty	1
18.	Vellalaviduthi	12
	Total	**203**

Source: Records, DRDA, Pudukkottai District.

Table 2.15 : Village Panchayatwise details of the allocation of IAY houses of Thiruvarankulam Union 2002-2003

Sl. No.	Name of the Village Panchayat	Total No. of houses sanctioned
1.	Alangadu	10
2.	Arayapatti	11
3.	Isugupatti	10
4.	Kothamangalam	17
5.	Kulamangalam (North)	10
6.	Melathur	25
7.	Palaiyur	10
8.	S.Kulavaipatti	2
9.	Sendhankudi	8
10.	Senthakudi	10
11.	Seriyalur Inam	10
12.	Thirukkatalai	7
13.	Vadakadu	15
14.	Venkidakulam	20
15.	Vennavalkudi	5
	Total	**170**

Source: Records, DRDA, Pudukkottai District.

Innovations

In order to obtain maximum benefits and achieve better results the guidelines of the IAY have incorporated some flexibility provisions and within this framework the Pudukkottai District administration successfully tried some innovations which ultimately resulted in greater efficiency, legitimacy and credibility of the system with effective stakeholders' participation. People were enthusiastic and started resorting to their own ways in designing, procuring materials and constructing the houses. By allowing the stakeholders to make their own choices, it was felt that the houses could be constructed in a way removing the social stigma of beneficiary-houses. There were major savings in cost and, by adopting this approach, it might be possible to pre-empt the occasional scenes of abandoned houses on the roadsides. In Pudukkottai District, when a chance was given to build their own houses with the money given, the beneficiaries went around fetching material like sand from nearby riverbeds, carrying it in headloads. The reduction in cost was visible. The contractor usually does the same work of getting the sand, granite and bricks at a price. Now the poor owner got granitc from nearby quarries by bargaining with the quarry owners known to him. When the work began, a relative of a beneficiary who was a good mason reached the place. He stayed on till the work was over. It was a reciprocal relationship because this man goes to him when the other has a need. That is a tradition in this region. Another neighbour helped through physical work and the work moved on. It went on at a slow pace and owner also attended to his routine work, completing the small things when he had leisure. The whole family lent a hand. Not only his family but also the whole neighbourhood helped each other in the process of completing their dream house. A sample case is described in Box 1.

Box 1: Sivanthalingapuram Experiment

Sivanthalingapuram hamlet, which comes under Semboothi Gram Panchayat, is located in Ponnmaravathi Block. Totally 15 IAY houses were allocated to this Panchayat, out of which 10 houses were constructed in Sivanthalingapuram. Nearly 30 families are residing in this area and all are immigrants from Piranmalai who came here with their kith and kin in search of jobs and have been settled here for about 30 years. This is a small hamlet with 30 houses including the new IAY houses, one street light, one hand pump, one TV room and one small temple where there is an occasion once in 3 years for celebration. This hamlet is situated on the road to Ponnamaravathy. There is no need to worry about transportation facility since all in the buses that pass by stop here considering the need. No other basic facility is available in this hamlet.

Initially they were forced to shift to the Adidravidar Colony of Semboothi Panchayat but they were very much stubborn about residing in the same place and they succeeded in their attempt by bringing the IAY scheme to their place twice, once in 1995-1996 and then in 2002-2003. This was made possible only because of their initiative. From getting patta for poramboke land to the construction of houses they faced several problems and finally they triumphed in their attempt. Their aspirations were made a reality by their sheer hard work and conscientious effort. The feeling of oneness was the subtle quality witnessed in this hamlet. This was further proved when they carried out the house construction in 2002-2003 under the IAY scheme. Out of 10 beneficiaries chosen for IAY houses five were masons. After receiving the work order they started constructing their houses collectively and completed the houses within

6 months. All the ten families worked for all the ten houses, choosing their own design. Since 5 were masons there was no need for technical assistance during the construction. All worked collectively and all the family members got involved in the construction work. Out of the 10 beneficiaries one was working in Chennai on a monthly salary. So it was not possible for him go over here during the construction. But the other family members helped his wife in the construction work. This is a rare phenomenon in urban areas but a peculiar characteristic which is still sustained among the rural masses. The concept of collective action is still alive in rural India. Some worked even in the night time because in the day time they worked as coolies to earn wages to earn bread for their family. They also felt that the rice given by the government during house construction and as a part of the IAY scheme was very much helpful because they did not need to worry during their non-wage days due to the construction activity. Even though the money allotted for each IAY house was Rs.32,000 they spent nearly Rs.70,000. They attached staircases and many other facilities according to their needs. They wanted their houses to be different from the earlier group houses. Houses which were constructed in 1995-96 under the same IAY scheme were handed to the contractors and all the houses look alike with a tapering roof 6 feet high. Under the new IAY scheme, which allows the beneficiary to design his house according to his requirements, the beneficiaries of Sivanthalingapuram constructed houses with roofs 9 ½ feet high and designed their houses suiting their aesthetic sense. Now the old IAY houses look awkward in front of these new IAY houses. This hamelt now serves as a model. Even the Nagaipattinam Additional Collector, Tuticorin District Sub Collector, Karur District Project Officer, DRDA, Virudhunagar and District Project Officer, DRDA visited this place to look at the involvement of the people and this model was considered a great success for the organized skill of the community. All the ten houses were built in a row and the locality looks beautiful with a newly laid mud road and coconut saplings and flower bearing plants planted in front of each house. One arduous effort made by the beneficiaries is worth mentioning here. There was only one hand pump located in this area. They had to pump day and night to get water for building and curing. This one hand pump served the needs of 30 families besides supplying water for construction of 10 houses. This was the only difficulty they experienced during the construction of their houses. Apart from this the beneficiaries were very much thankful to the officials for their facilitating role. Making the beneficiaries build their own houses and permitting the users to have their own designs in tune with local conditions makes them feel a sense of belonging which will pre-empt the frequent demands for repairs. This will be definitely proved in the case of Sivanthalingapuram.

The DRDA, Pudukkottai, initiated a major attempt to popularize the stabilized mud block technology and a number of equipments were purchased from Auroville, Pondicherry. The technology was introduced to the Indira Awas Yojana housing groups and many opted to go in for it. Women have also been trained in the technology and also in masonry for long term sustainability. So rural women are now building their own houses. This happened in Melathur Panchayat in Thirvarankulam Block. Here 25 houses have been built and as many as 100 houses are expected to be completed soon with the new technology. The houses allotted for the year 2003-2004 are to be constructed with the mud block technology. Work orders have been issued to those who have opted to construct houses with mud blocks. This technology saves from 30 to 40 per cent on the cost and these are extremely eco-friendly houses. Tank silt, mostly collected during the desiltation work under various programmes, is used to make earthern blocks which are found to be hardy for the purpose. For the coming year 2003-2004, the DRDA has purchased 6 equipments to produce stabilized mud blocks. The Melathur experiment convinced the beneficiaries to opt for the mud block technology. Box 2 describes the Melathur experiment.

Box 2: Melathur Experiment

The Melathur Panchayat President, Mr.Saravanan, was elected for the first time in a close contest. He is a mechanical engineer by profession. He hails from an educated family with a keen commitment to social service. Earlier he worked in an industry located in Tiruchirapalli and was paid highly. He left his lucarative job to be sworn in as Village Panchayat President. When his Panchayat was allocated 25 houses to be constructed under the IAY scheme, his technological acumen started working. He had heard of a story told by the villagers about the quality of the mud available in a tank situated in their Panchayat. Earthern pots made out of this mud possessed the quality of endurance without any damage. So he decided to use the mud for constructing the IAY houses. His idea was further channellized by the Project Officer, DRDA, Pudukkottai, by informing him about the equipment for producing mud blocks, which was available in Auroville, Pondicherry. Rs.42,000 was paid by the DRDA to procure the equipment which was handed over to the Panchayat. In order to satisfy the beneficiaries and clear their doubts about the quality of the mud blocks, Mr.Saravanan took all the 25 beneficiaries to Auroville to see the multistoried buildings constructed out of mud blocks and thereby their endurance and capacity was proved. Returning satisfied, the beneficiaries were given training in producing mud blocks with the mud dug up from the good old tank in their village. All the houses were now built with the mud blocks. In order to meet the need for a large quantity of mud blocks, Mr.Saravanan, being an engineer, designed a mud block producing equipment on his own at a low cost of Rs.20,000 only. It became convenient for the beneficiaries to produce more mud blocks quickly with the two equipments. The production cost of a single block costs Rs.1.20 and a double block costs Rs.2.40. To construct a 9 foot high house with a minimum plinth area of 210 sq. ft. 1400 mud blocks are enough. Every day the beneficiary can produce 350 bocks to 500 blocks depending upon his convenience. Therefore three days will be enough to produce the mud blocks required for a single house. Some users produced them on their own, minimizing the labour cost. Others employed labourers to mould mud blocks for a wage of Rs.70 and Rs.30 for men and women respectively. Curing work is done for 21 days by spraying water on the block in order to strengthen its durability further. Using this mud block technology the user can construct his house within the money given by the government.

The initiative taken by the President and the facility provided by the officials have introduced a major innovation in building houses at minimum cost. Seeing this, other Panchayat Presidents have brought the beneficiaries of IAY houses of their Panchayats to look at the houses constructed with the mud block technology. Now a training programme is in progress in Pudukkottai District for constructing houses at minimum cost using this technology. The Secretary to Government for Rural Development, Government of Tamil Nadu, Ms.Shanta Sheela Nair issued a circular to all the districts to adopt the Melathur experiment.

The DRDA is also motivating self help groups (SHGs) to buy the mud block equipment and this may help them to generate more income because more work orders have been issued to construct houses using mud blocks. Training has also been given to them and the Panchayat Presidents are being motivated to buy the equipment. A subsidy for procuring the equipment is also under consideration. In places like Pudukkottai, with a profusion of tanks, the tank sediment can be used for making mud blocks. The limited dependence on the official machinery will help save the beneficiary from the procedural delays including the fluctuations in cement supply. In general this approach will be highly eco-friendly as the use of cement and other energy intensive technologies is limited.

Changing the seemingly stagnant traditional approach has paid rich dividends in Pudukkottai. The mud block procedure of stipulated measurements has been transformed by the introduction of a new set of procedures with sufficient flexibility and made available in Tamil to the users bringing in transparency. Work orders are issued to the beneficiaries themselves. This has stopped the beneficiaries raising questions of accountability, leaving less space for misuse. While retaining the general conditions like plinth area, many other stringent provisions like measurements for windows etc. have been waived enabling the users to have their own designs. The users are also free to procure various items unlike earlier when there were specific stipulations. So the users, in many cases, went in for provisions like staircases to go to the terraces and additions meant for animals etc. Box 3 explains the different design types adopted in the construction of IAY houses.

Box 3: Different Design Types

Mr.Perumal, 35, is one among the eight IAY beneficiaries of Vathanakottai in Kunnandarkoil Block. In spite of being a seasonal employee he was in a position to spend Rs.45,000 extra for his house to ensure a grand appearance. His wife and his three children played effective roles during the construction and assisted Perumal in all ways. Their hard work brought results in the form of an affluent house with a drawing room, kitchen, bedroom, attached toilet and staircase. Well designed windows and front doors were installed in his house. He also feels that he has attained a social status by having a beautiful house of his own. He said, "Ennoda mathipum en kulandhaikalukku naan cherthu vaikira chothum indha veedu dhan" (I am saving respect and property for my children through this house). He feels relaxed and satisfied that his house won't be identified as a government group house.

Another case is very much interesting in Valamangalam Panchayat of the same block. In this case two brothers were allotted IAY houses considering their poor condition. Their plots were adjacent to each other's. So they decided to construct their houses with a common wall which might serve as a partition for the two houses, thereby saving on cost since they could not afford to spend money other than the money given by the government. Using the flexibility provision they now have houses in their name which they couldn't dream of earlier.

Even though construction of a staircase can cost around 5,000 many are opting for it. In Thalampatti hamlet of Parambur Panchayat in Annavasal Block, two beneficiaries decided to have a single common staircase attached to their two houses. Through this arrangement they could save money and adjustment could be made between them.

In Mookampatti Panchayat, Pudukkottai Union, Ms.Selvam, in spite of space constraints constructed her house suiting all her needs. She is a vegetable vendor and keeps poultry. She found space under the staircase of her IAY house to construct a cage to keep her poultry safe. The design she adopted was a welcome move and others have followed this pattern seeing the resultant convenience.

Apart from these designs, many have decorated their floor, installed a small partition inside their house to use as either a kitchen or a bedroom, built shelves to keep things and lofts for storage, and included concealed wiring.

All these were made possible only by the flexibility provisions adopted by the district administration. There are other advantages in this arrangement, like the house owner identifying the house as his own. It is common practice that the beneficiaries of government houses consider the house a government house for even minor repairs. It is possible to reduce the cost drastically if the future owners, even if they are poor, are entrusted with the construction which will also save a lot of effort on the part of officers and staff.

Achievements

Out of 1781 houses taken up in 2002-2003, 1685 houses have been completed. The shortage of 96 houses was mainly due to some procedural delay in giving work orders. In previous years the construction was 100 per cent in Pudukkottai District.

Impact of the Scheme

Shelter is one among the important basic needs of the people. For the poverty stricken rural masses even finding shelter with minimum requirements is a dream. The Government of India has come to their rescue by providing houses. Normally in government housing schemes the government hands over houses built in the same design to the needy groups. Routine procedures and measurements make the government houses easy to identify and the quality of the houses is also very poor. In Pudukkottai, the District Rural Development Agency (DRDA) allowed the beneficiaries to construct houses of their own using their own design and resources and as a result one finds a major change. The original type of group houses is only a conception of the engineers who have no experience of rural life.

The abandoned group houses on the roadside show that construction by contractors often results in cracks in walls, broken windows, roof damage and so on. Therefore handing over the task to the beneficiaries themselves will bring about a drastic change as the experiment in of Pudukkottai shows dramatic results. People were enthusiastic and started making use of their own ways to construct *homes and not houses.* Being the owner, the beneficiary will take more care in construction also so that it serves him for a long period of time. The impact created by the innovations adopted in housing construction are explained in the following pages.

Psychological Impact

Houses constructed under the earlier IAY scheme for SCs/STs in groups are clearly different from other ordinary houses. Now, under the new scheme, the beneficiaries are allowed to have their own design. So, now they feel that their houses cannot be identified as houses given by the government free of cost. Outsiders cannot identify their houses as meant for SCs/STs as in earlier cases. They also feel that they have attained a status by owning a house suiting their requirements. Also they think that their position has been elevated and they can be on par with the other communities in society. This kind of psychological upliftment will be a great success for the government, because, thereafter, equality won't be a distant dream. The attitude and behaviour of the beneficiaries is also changing and their drive for elevation from their lower status is becoming fruitful.

Sociological Impact

Most of the beneficiaries are happy that their house now does not look like a government house with tapering roof as in the old model. It is a normal house like any other house. They realize that through this they have attained a social status and they also feel that they will be respected in society. Many have done their house warming ceremony grandly inviting their relatives, friends and neighbours to their house. They are very much proud of having a wonderful house and the sense of belonging is now much higher. They do not want to give any impression to others that this house was given by the government.

Economic Impact

The beneficiary was involved from the construction of the basement to the completion of the house. So he knows the expense incurred at every stage. Since he himself was involved in the labour he knows how much he saved because of his labour contribution. Further many have borrowed money from moneylenders initially to construct their house beautifully. So they will be working hard in the future to pay the money back. This has inculcated in them the concept of hard work. Some have used their savings for the construction. This has taught them the use of savings and they will do the same in the future also. Apart from this they have learned a lot from cost effective technology to optimum utilization of resources by constructing the houses on their own.

Ownership

The concept of ownership of the project, even though aided by the government, was introduced in the mindset of the beneficiary by making him involve himself in all the stages of the construction. He was made to feel that he was the major stakeholder of the scheme and the government served him only as a facilitator. The opinion from the official side was that the time of the officials was saved, because, when the task is left to the beneficiaries they will do it correctly and therefore only monitoring need be done by the officials. They need not spend much time on this and can concentrate on some other work. From the official point of view, due to the flexibility in procedures and change in government policy, the following benefits have emerged from the project:

— The reduction of bureaucratic rules and hierarchies.

— Budget transparency and ability to identify the cost inputs and outputs.

— Segregation of organizations and their functions, introducing purchaser/provider distinction.

— Increased provider competition.

— Increased consumer power through enhanced scope for exit and redress.

Salient Features

The salient features of the IAY scheme, with its flexibility provisions, can be outlined as hereunder:

(1) Since beneficiaries are directly involved in the construction of their own houses instead of entrusting it to intermediaries (contractors, Panchayat Presidents and Union Councillors) the concept of ownership is inculcated and hence the beneficiary is considered a major stakeholder or development participant and the role of the government is confined to that of a facilitator providing monetary assistance only. To substantiate this view two cases are explained in Box 4.

Box 4: Thalampatti and Perumanadu Experiments

Professional masons of Thalampatti hamlet, Parambur Panchayat, constructed IAY houses on their own near a forest area. Both manual labour and masonary work were done by them without paying a single rupee to outsiders. There were several conditions which forced them to work on their own. First, they were too poor to pay others for the construction work. Secondly, since it was their own house, they said they would work better without bothering about any constraint, so that they could construct the house on their own and according to their needs and taste. Thirdly they said that because of their distant location near the forest they themselves had to work since nobody would come from outside to work for them. They converted their constraints and hurdles into advantages and considered it an opportunity for their upliftment making them property holders through their hard work. This was made possible by the flexibility provisions in the guidelines and the administration has enabled the beneficiaries to become stakeholders in the scheme.

Another case from Perumanadu Panchayat of Annavasal Union illustrates the same phenomenon. Mr.Pichaikani, a hearing impaired Muslim, constructed a beautiful house despite his physical disability. Possessing a house of his own was his long cherished desire and now it has come true because of his persistence. He thanked the Perumanadu Panchayat President Mr.Senbagam Natesan for his constant support and for selecting him as an IAY beneficiary. One thing he felt sorry about was that he was forced to sell his cow to mobilize money for the construction. But later he consoled himself saying that the house will be useful not only to him but also to his children. In order to have a house in his name he has taken many extreme steps and risks. His desire was mainly to become a stakeholder.

(2) As per the guidelines the construction area should be a minimum of 210 square feet and the house should have a toilet, smokeless chulha and rainwater harvesting structure as stipulated by the administration. If the above are conformed to the design of the house, building materials, construction and labour are left to the beneficiary's discretion.

Box 5: Punakulam and Melathur Experiments

The Pudukkottai District administration has taken accelerated steps for the installation of rainwater harvesting structures. The Punakulam Panchayat of Gandarvakottai Union was adopted by a pipe industry to install rainwater harvesting structures in all the buildings of the Panchayat. This was encouraged by the district administration. Further, Mr.Saravanan, Melathur Panchayat President, has taken steps to provide rainwater harvesting system to all the households in his Panchayat. The beneficiaries of IAY houses were given the full amount only after checking the provision of rainwater collection structures. Stress was laid not only on rainwater harvesting but also on toilet facilities. The district has been chosen for the provision of toilet facilities to IAY beneficiaries also. Considering the health of women and fuel conservation the use of smokeless chula is also stressed. The targets can be easily achieved by the administration by making the IAY beneficiaries adopt these provisions. The rainwater harvesting initiative was taken much earlier to the announcement of the government to have rainwater harvesting structure in each and every house and building compulsorily.

(3) The introduction of mud block technology to the beneficiaries saves 30 per cent to 40 per cent on cost and the experiment in Melathur proved that houses can be constructed within the amount given by the government.

Box 6: A Poor Coolie's Experience

Kajamohideen, 33, was one of the beneficiaries of the IAY scheme in Melathur Panchayat. He built his house using mud blocks at minimum cost. Being a coolie he could not afford any other technology for house construction. He worked with other users to prepare mud blocks and opted for a tapering roof rather than a flat roof since it could further reduce the cost of construction. The mud block technology came in handy for this poor beneficiary to construct his house on his own within the money allotted by the government. All the other users of IAY houses of this Panchayat also benefited from this technology.

Apart from construction of IAY houses toilets have also been constructed using mud blocks cheaply under the total rural sanitation programme. Thus the introduction of this technology serves several purposes.

(4) From producing mud blocks to masonry, beneficiary families get involved in the labour work. Since most of the beneficiaries are daily wage earners, the rice given by the government as a part of the IAY scheme makes them feel secure during their non-wage days while they are involved in the house construction.

Box 7: Economy and Hard Work

As already mentioned the beneficiaries of IAY houses get Rs.32,000 each from the government. But the whole amount is not paid in cash: 500 kg of rice is given to them at a price of Rs.5.65 per kg and the total cost, namely, Rs.2,825, is deducted from the grant of Rs.32,000. The idea behind giving rice to the users is that, since the poor beneficiary is going to be involved in the construction process, as it is not left to contractors, he has to lose his daily wages since most of them are coolies. So, to meet the need for food for the family, rice is given to them. What is peculiar is that some daily wages beneficiaries work in the daytime as coolies and work on their houses in the evening and at night. Mr.Arumugam, who hails from Thiruvengaivasal Panchayat, who constructed an IAY house in the name of his wife Ms.Rajalakshmi, said that he constructed his house only by working in the evening. In the morning he worked as a coolie in spite of the rice given by the government. The wage he earned was useful for the construction and enabled him to have a house with all facilities and also looking beautiful. The concept of ownership inculcated in him the tendency to work hard.

(5) A booklet on IAY guidelines was given to each and every user by the DRDA, Pudukkottai. This booklet gives them all information for cost effective construction which will be very much useful to the users.

Box No. 8: Transparency in Information Dissemination

This booklet gives information about the objectives of the IAY scheme, the selection of beneficiaries, the salient features of the scheme, allocation of grant, construction area, who has to construct, how to construct and some general information about environmental protection. According to the information in this book a Task Force Committee will be appointed to select the beneficiaries and later the selected beneficiaries list will be approved through the Gram Sabha. The Task Force Committee consists of the concerned Panchayat President, the Panchayat members and the Block Development Officer (BDO) or some other officer nominated by the BDO. The booklet also gives information about the cost effective method for quality construction. The details are given here under:

Construction Cost

Sl. No.	Construction Cost (for 210 sq ft)	Amount Estimated		
		Scale	Cost	Amount
1.	Basement	11.60	42.00	487.00
2.	Filling sand for basement	3.16	146.80	464.00
3.	Sand, stone, cement for basement	3.16	1150.00	3634.00
4.	Small stones and cement	3.40	1090.60	3708.00
5.	Bricks and cement	10.65	1257.50	13392.00
6.	Roof, shelf, slabs	2.73	1980.00	5405.00
7.	Iron rods	145 kg	20.50	2973.00
8.	Roof ceiling	45sq m	48.00	2160.00
9.	Plastering the house with cement (ratio 1:5)	114 sq m	38.00	4332.00
10.	Iron door (2.00 m 0.09 m)	1 No.	1044.00	1044.00
11.	Door for toilet	1 No.	473.00	473.00
12.	Window (iron/R.C.C.)	2.43 sq m	160.00	389.00
13.	Limestone for white washing (two times)	89 sq m	5.00	445.00
14.	Colour wash (two times)	55 sq m	6.00	330.00
15.	Paint for iron door	6.30 sq m	56.00	353.00
16.	Basin for toilet and other sanitary accessories	L.S.		250.00
17.	Fitting of doors and windows	L.S.	120.00	120.00
18.	Smokeless Chulha	L.S.	200.00	200.00
19.	Writing the name of beneficiary on the wall and lock & key	L.S.	150.00	150.00
20.	Centring cost	20.63	150.00	3095.00
21.	Miscellaneous			96.00
	Total			**43,500.00**

(6) The district administration, by adopting the flexibility provisions, has even allowed two beneficiaries to construct combined houses with one partition which cost them less and also two houses with one common staircase due to space constraints.

(7) In earlier government houses the toilet was provided within the house, which made the users feel uneasy about using the toilet and made them use the toilet as a store room or to keep poultry or firewood. As per the new guidelines the beneficiary can have the toilet at any place convenient to him so that the beneficiary uses it without much problem.

Box 9: Old Vs New IAY Houses

In Onangudi Panchayat the old type of IAY houses were constructed in 1990-91 and now new IAY houses (2002-2003) have been constructed opposite them. Ms. Jegathambal is one of the beneficiaries of new IAY houses and her cousin Ms.Vijayakumari is the beneficiary of an old IAY house. Ms.Vijayakumari uses her latrine as a storeroom to store firewood. Her family members are reluctant to use the toilet because their kitchen and toilet are situated adjacent to each other. But Ms.Jegathambal has constructed the toilet a few yards behind her house. As per the guidelines there should be a toilet but it can be anywhere within the house premises. Jegathambal, an illiterate now learning through "Mahalir Thittam Arivoli", assured that she and her family members will use the toilet. She has also permitted Ms.Vijayakumari to use her toilet without any inhibition. Ms.Vijayakumari, even though educated, could not convince her family members to use the toilet within her house. But the new provision makes everyone use the toilet.

(8) Finally, permitting the users' own design and construction process enables them to construct their house strongly because of which they may not incur cost of repairs in future. It has been proved in Pudukkottai that it is better to let the owners build their houses, may be with a little supervision. By entrusting the construction to the owners themselves the time of a big army of officials can be saved. Wherever beneficiaries constructed their houses under this scheme on their own, for repair work they won't come to the government as they declare that they are the owners. They have also invested money.

Points for Consideration

To be impartial and objective in the evaluation process some limitations were also identified in the implementation of the IAY scheme. They are listed hereunder and explained with suitable cases:

(1) Since the beneficiaries are allowed to construct houses of their own design some are not in a position to construct within the stipulated time span. Officials regard this as delay. Out of 1781 houses taken up in 2002-2003, 1685 houses have been completed so far. 5.4 per cent of the people couldn't finish within the stipulated time (during 2001-2002 100 per cent completion was recorded). But when this was referred to the District Collector he said that it was so not because of allowing the beneficiaries to construct the houses. Any construction whether undertaken by beneficiaries or by contractors will take the same time to be completed. In these cases construction was delayed only due to the delay in the movement of the files in the office.

(2) The minimum area for construction is 210 sq. ft. as per the guidelines. But many have constructed more than 300 sq. ft. and it has cost them more than Rs. 1 lakh, landing them in misery.

Box 10 : A Case of Overreaching

Mr. Natesan (60) of Illaikadaviduthi Panchayat of Karambakudi Union, the father of 2 sons and 2 daughters, was very much happy as soon he was selected a beneficiary of the IAY scheme. So he decided to construct a house containing 3 portions so that it would be useful for his sons to settle down without any dispute. He possessed a pair of oxen and one acre of land. Since as per the blueprint of his house the estimaed cost was more than one lakh rupees he decided to borrow money from his brother-in-law who was in Malaysia. But the brother-in-law gave only a small amount. So, Mr. Natesan was forced to sell his land and oxen to get money to complete the house. Even though he consoles himself saying that he has constructed a pucca house, he feels very badly about the circumstances that led him to sell his land and oxen.

Looking at similar cases now it has been decided that the minimum plinth area for construction can be exceeded by only 15 sq. ft. This condition is now mentioned in the work order itself. Further the beneficiaries are also not allowed to construct staircases because it costs them nearly Rs.5,000 which may be otherwise useful. But they can undertake further construction after the completion of the minimum requirements as mentioned in the work order. These are some of the changes made in 2003-2004 work order.

(3) Some beneficiaries felt that the grant given by the government is not sufficient and so they are forced to sell their cattle and land and borrow money from moneylenders at high rates of interest, which lands them in debt.

Box 11: A Sad Tale

Keelacheri Panchayat of Avudayarkoil Block was allotted 20 houses under the IAY scheme. Mrs.Ganesan was one of the beneficiaries. She constructed her house at a cost of Rs.10,000 over and above the grant from the government in Kodugavayal hamlet. She says, "The information brochure given by the district administration itself estimates that the cost of house construction will be around Rs.43,000. But the money allotted is only Rs.32,000. My husband, being a mason, will have employment only for 150 days in a year. With his meagre income and 3 children we were not in a position to spend Rs.10,000 extra. But to complete the house we were forced to borrow money from a moneylender at a high rate of interest. I am now very much scared and worried about how to pay the money back with interest".

(4) Another important thing to note is that even though a toilet was made mandatory under the scheme its usage is still doubtful in a few places. Needed awareness should be given to the people about the merits of using toilet and also about the disadvantages of open air defecation. But from the coming year (2003-04) the administration has decided to withhold Rs.2000 from the last instalment of grant to ensure that the beneficiaries use the toilet. This will make them use the toilets, the administration hopes.

(5) Provision of chula is not welcomed by the users and after getting the full amount of money the chulha is removed and not used. The needed awareness is not given.

Box 12: Difficulties with the Smokeless Chula

The fitting of smokeless chulha was insisted upon by the government officials. Ms.Nallathangal of Valamangalam Panchayat too fitted the chulha in her house, but, after getting the full amount from the government, she took the chulha from inside the house and left it outside, because she feared that the smoke from the chulha would spoil the beauty of her house with coatings of carbon. The District Collector feels that, with regard to the smokeless chulha, the usefulness depends on the wind direction: sometimes it may cause suffocation inside the house. So, from the coming financial year (2003-2004), the beneficiary will be given the choice of installation of the chula anywhere around the house, considering their comfort, so that it will be useful to them.

(6) Finally some other infrastructure facilities like road, electricity and drinking water may also be considered. If the houses are in groups, on the part of government, it will be easy for them to provide infrastructure facilities like road and drinking water supply. But this was possible only in a few places like Sivanthalingapuram, Thalampatti etc. In other places most of the houses are located in different places and not in one street. Therefore provision of these facilities will be difficult. However, after completion of the construction, the BDO will forward an application to the Electricity Board and all the beneficiaries will be provided with electricity supply.

In spite of these considerations positive steps have been taken by the district administration to ensure the participation of the people in the process of development. A considerable reorientation of the administrative system has been done. To improve Public Service Management, the need for change leading to creating a synergy between the public and the private sectors, developing an administrative structure which is transparent and open, harnessing information and reorienting the staff towards better performance and combating political and administrative corruption have become aspects of the new perspective. Most of the countries have attempted to limit the role of the state through downsizing of the bureaucracy, devolution of authority, cost reduction, contracting out some of the operative functions of the government, developing and designing result oriented appraisal systems, and commercialization as well as market orientation of governmental activities. This has been supported by effective accountability achieved through an open reporting system. The administration is apparently moving towards result orientation from rule orientation, from systems to enterprise, obedience to reward, inaction to action, centralization to decentralization and the duties of administrators to the rights of citizens. Through this the traditional public administration approach is being replaced by the Public Management approach. This new phase in governance reflects the insertion of a management perspective into public organizations. Efficiency is considered more important than rule obedience, effectiveness comes before legality, and, flexibility and adoption are more vital than predictability and responsibility. In Pudukkottai, the district administration has incorporated these provisions while implementing the government schemes and thereby achieved the maximum.

Table 2.16 : Allotment of IAY New Houses for the Year 2003-2004

Sl. No.	Name of the Block	Allotment of IAY New Houses to the following categories						
		Freed bonded labour	Affected by riot	Widows	Fire Victims	Ex-service men	PH	Total
1.	Annavasal			20			11	31
2.	Arimalam			23	4	2	7	36
3.	Kunnan-darkoil			23	1	1	11	36
4.	Ponnama-ravathi			20	2	1	19	42
5.	Pudukkottai			25	1		10	36
6.	Thirumayam			18	3	2	22	45
7.	Viralimalai			27	39	12	17	95
8.	Aranthangi		1	37	8		21	67
9.	Avudayar koil	7		23	4	1	11	46
10.	Gandarva kottai			21	1		7	29
11.	Karambakkudi		4	17	28	5	13	67
12.	Manamelkudi	5		22			7	34
13.	Thirvarankulam	7		28	4	1	20	60
	Total	19	5	304	95	25	176	624

Source: Records, DRDA, Pudukkottai District.

Table 2.17 : Village Panchayatwise details of the allocation of IAY houses of Annavasal Union 2003–2004

Sl. No.	Name of the Panchayat	Categories						
		Freed bonded labour	Affected by riot	Widows	Fire Victims	Ex-service men	PH	Total
1.	Ariyur			2				2
2.	Kathavampatti			1				1
3.	Khothiarapatti			2				2
4.	Madakiyanallur			2			3	5
5.	Perumanadu			1			2	3
6.	Poongudi			2			1	3
7.	Pulvayal			2			3	5
8.	Rapoosal			1			1	2
9.	Thalinji			2				2
10.	Thirunallur						1	1
11.	Thiruvangaivasal			2				2
12.	Vellanur			3				3
	Total			20			11	31

Source: Records, DRDA, Pudukkottai District.

Table 2.18 : Village Panchayatwise details of the allocation of IAY Houses of Arimalam Union 2003–2004

Sl. No.	Name of the Panchayat	Categories						
		Freed bonded labour	Affected by riot	Widows	Fire Victims	Ex-service men	PH	Total
1.	Ayinkudi			4				4
2.	Embal						3	3
3.	K. Chettipatti				3		1	4
4.	Kadayakkudi			4			2	6
5.	Kadiyappatti			2		1		3
6.	Kaikulanvayal						1	1
7.	Kannagarakkudi			3				3
8.	Karamanglam			3				3
9.	Mirattuniali			3				3
10.	Piliyavayal			1				1
11.	Samuthiram			1				1
12.	Sengeerai			2	1			3
13.	Valavamanikam					1		1
	Total			23	4	2	7	36

Source: Records, DRDA, Pudukkottai District.

Table 2.19 : Village Panchayatwise details of the allocation of IAY Houses of Kunnandarkoil Union 2003–2004

Sl. No.	Name of the Panchayat	Categories						
		Freed bonded labour	Affected by riot	Widows	Fire Victims	Ex service men	PH	Total
1.	Andakkulam			2				2
2.	Chettipatti			1				1
3.	Kannanagudi			1			3	4
4.	Killukkottai						1	1
5.	Mangadevanpatti						4	4
6.	Minthur			1				1
7.	Puliyur			4			1	5
8.	Sengalur			2				2
9.	Thennangudi			1				1
10.	Vaithur			2				2
11.	Valamangalam			5		1	2	8
12.	Valiyampatti			2				2
13.	Vathanakottai				1			1
14.	Vathnakurichi			2				2
	Total			23	1	1	11	36

Source: Records, DRDA, Pudukkottai District.

Table 2.20 : Village Panchayatwise details of the allocation of IAY Houses of Ponnamaravathi Union 2003–2004

Sl. No.	Name of the Panchayat	Categories						
		Freed bonded labour	Affected by riot	Widows	Fire Victims	Ex-service men	PH	Total
1.	Aalampatti			5				5
2.	Arasamalai			2			4	6
3.	Odayathur				1		5	6
4.	Gudalur			2				2
5.	Kataiyur						1	1
6.	Kattupatti					1		1
7.	Konnayampatti			1				1
8.	Mulathaniyam			1	1		1	3
9.	R. Palakurichi			3				3
10.	Seranur			1				1
11.	Thoothur			3			2	5
12.	Thottiyampatti			2				2
13.	Valakuruchi						6	6
	Total			20	2	1	19	42

Source: Records, DRDA, Pudukkottai District.

Table 2.21 : Village Panchayatwise details of the allocation of IAY Houses of Pudukkottai Union 2003–2004

Sl. No.	Name of the Panchayat	Categories						
		Freed bonded labour	Affected by riot	Widows	Fire Victims	Ex-service men	PH	Total
1.	9A Nathampattai						1	1
2.	9B Nathampannai			4				4
3.	Karuppudayanpatti			5				5
4.	Kuppayampatti						2	2
5.	Manaviduthi			2	1		3	6
6.	Muthur			5			1	6
7.	Perungalur						2	2
8.	Perungoodan-viduthi			3				3
9.	Puthambur			3				3
10.	Sembattue						1	1
11.	Vadavalam			2				2
12.	Vagavasal			1				1
	Total			25	1		10	36

Source: Records, DRDA, Pudukkottai District.

Table 2.22 : Village Panchayatwise details of the allocation of IAY Houses of Thirumayam Union 2003–2004

Sl. No.	Name of the Panchayat	Categories						
		Freed bonded labour	Affected by riot	Widows	Fire Victims	Ex-servicemen	PH	Total
1.	Adhanur						1	1
2.	Aranginampatti				1	2		3
3.	Elanjavur						1	1
4.	Kannanur			1	1		1	3
5.	Konnapattu						2	2
6.	Kulippirai			1			1	2
7.	Kuruvikodanpatti			1				1
8.	Lembalakkudi			3				
9.	Melur			2				2
10.	Mithilaipatti						3	3
11.	Neikkonam						1	1
12.	Neivasal			3			4	7
13.	P. Alayapuri			1				1
14.	Panayapatti						1	1
15.	Peraiyur						1	1
16.	Rangiyam						1	1
17.	Rarapuram				1		1	2
18.	Sethurappatti						2	2
19.	Thirumayam			3			2	5
20.	Thulayanur			3				3
	Total			18	3	2	22	45

Source: Records; DRDA, Pudukkottai District.

Table 2.23 : Village Panchayatwise details of the allocation of IAY Houses of Viralimalai Union 2003–2004

Sl. No.	Name of the Panchayat	Categories						
		Freed bonded labour	Affected by riot	Widows	Fire Victims	Ex-service men	PH	Total
1.	Agarapatti				7			7
2.	Alangudi			1	1			2
3.	Avur				1	2		3
4.	Boothakkudi				3		2	5
5.	Kalamvur					1	3	4
6.	Kalkudi			2	2			4
7.	Kasavanur				3	2		5
8.	Kathalur					2		2
9.	Kodambalur			5			2	7
10.	Komangalam			4				4
11.	Lakshamanapathi				4			4
12.	Mandaiyur			2				2
13.	Maruthampatti				2			2
14.	Matthur				4			4

Table 2.23 : *(Contd.)*

Sl. No.	Name of the Panchayat	Categories						
		Freed bonded labour	Affected by riot	Widows	Fire Victims	Ex-servicemen	PH	Total
15.	Meenaveku						1	1
16.	Nangupatti						5	5
17.	Neerapalani			4	1			5
18.	Palandampatti				2		2	4
19.	Permabur				1			1
20.	Poyyamani				2			2
21.	Rajagiri			4			1	5
22.	Thennambadi			2				2
23.	Thennathirayanpatti			2				2
24.	Theravur				4			4
25.	Thondamanalur			1			1	2
26.	Vemmani					1		1
27.	Vilappatti					1		1
28.	Viralur				1	3		4
29.	Viruthapatti				1			1
	Total			27	39	12	17	95

Source: Records, DRDA, Pudukkottai District.

Table 2.24 : Village Panchayatwise details of the allocation of IAY Houses of Aranthangi Union 2003–2004

Sl. No.	Name of the Panchayat	Categories						
		Freed bonded labour	Affected by riot	Widows	Fire Victims	Ex-servicemen	PH	Total
1.	Alapiranthan			5				5
2.	Amarasimmendra-puram			4				4
3.	Arasarakulam Vadapatti			2				2
4.	Athani						2	2
5.	Eagaperumagular			2				2
6.	Eganivayal			5				5
7.	Idayar						1	1
8.	Kammangadu			3			2	5
9.	Keelkudiamman jackey						3	3
10.	Kodivayal			3			2	5
11.	Kongudi						1	1

Table 2.24 *(Contd.)*

Sl. No.	Name of the Panchayat	Categories						
		Freed bonded labour	Affected by riot	Widows	Fire Victims	Ex-servicemen	PH	Total
12.	Mangalandu			3				3
13.	Mangudi				1		1	2
14.	Mookkudi				2			2
15.	Narpuvalakkudi			2	2			4
16.	Nattumangalam			1			1	2
17.	Oorvani						1	1
18.	Poovathakkudi		1					1
19.	Ramasamyapuam				3		3	6
20.	Sunayakkadu			1			2	3
21.	Thanthani			3				3
22.	Vaembagudi East			3			2	5
	Total		1	37	8		21	67

Source: Records, DRDA, Pudukkottai District.

Table 2.25 : Village Panchayatwise details of the allocation of IAY Houses of Avudayarkoil Union 2003–2004

Sl. No.	Name of the Panchayat	Categories						
		Freed bonded labour	Affected by riot	Widows	Fire Victims	Ex-servicemen	PH	Total
1.	Karur			4	1			5
2.	Kathiramangalam				1			1
3.	Kavadukudi	2		2				4
4.	Mimisal			2			1	3
5.	Nattanipurasakudi						1	1
6.	Okkur						3	3
7.	Palavarasan			1				1
8.	Pandipathiram			1				1
9.	Porunavalur					1		1
10.	Ponbethi	4					1	5
11.	Punniyavayal			2	1			2
12.	Senganam							1
13.	Theeyur			3	1			3
14.	Thiruppunavasal						2	3
15.	Thondamanendal			3			1	4
16.	Velvarai			2				2
17.	Veeramanglam			3			2	5
18.	Vettanur	1						1
	Total	7		23	4	1	11	46

Source : Records, DRDA, Pudukkottai District.

Table 2.26 : Village Panchayatwise details of the allocation of IAYHouses of Gandarvakottai Union 2003-04.

Sl. No.	Name of the Panchayat	Categories						
		Freed bonded labour	Affected by riot	Widows	Fire Victims	Ex-servicemen	PH	Total
1.	Akkachipatti			1				1
2.	Andanur			1			1	2
3.	Gandarvakottai						1	1
4.	Komapuram						1	1
5.	Kurumpoondi			5				5
6.	Manganur			3				3
7.	Mattangal			2			1	3
8.	Nadupatti				1			1
9.	Neppugai			5				5
10.	Pudunagar			1				1
11.	Pudupatti						3	3
12.	Sunthampatti			3				3
	Total			21	1		7	29

Source : Records, DRDA, Pudukkottai District.

Table 2.27 : Village Panchayatwise details of the allocation of IAY Houses of Karambakudi Union 2003–2004

Sl. No.	Name of the Panchayat	Categories						
		Freed bonded labour	Affected by riot	Widows	Fire Victims	Ex-servicemen	PH	Total
1.	Banthuvakottai			1				1
2.	Kaliaranviduthi				2			2
3.	Kanakkankadu				3		2	5
4.	Karambaviduthi				1			1
5.	Karukeelatheru				2			2
6.	Karuppattipatti				3			3
7.	Kaattathi			1				1
8.	Keerathur		3					3
9.	Kulanthiranpatti			1			1	2
10.	Malaiyur		1		1		3	5
11.	Mankottai			2			2	4
12.	Maruthanconviduthi			5				5
13.	Mullankurichi				5		2	7
14.	Pallavaranpatti					2		3

Table 2.27 *(Contd.)*

Sl. No.	Name of the Panchayat	Categories						
		Freed bonded labour	Affected by riot	Widows	Fire Victims	Ex-servicemen	PH	Total
15.	Pilaviduthi			2			1	3
16.	Ponnanviduthi				1	1		2
17.	Rangiranviduthi				1			1
18.	Regunathapuram			3			2	5
19.	Sengamedu				2			2
20.	Vadatheru				1			1
21.	Valankondanviduthi					1		1
22.	Vanakkankadu				2			2
23.	Vandanviduthi			2	2	1		5
24.	Vellalaviduthi				1			1
	Total		4	17	28	5	13	67

Source: Records, DRDA, Pudukkottai District.

Table 2.28 : Village Panchayatwise details of the allocation of IAY Houses of Manamelkudi Union 2003–2004

Sl. No.	Name of the Panchayat	Categories						
		Freed bonded labour	Affected by riot	Widows	Fire Victims	Ex-servicemen	PH	Total
1.	Annapattianam						2	2
2.	Biramanavayal			2				2
3.	Edayathur	4		2				6
4.	Idayathimanglam			1				1
5.	Karahathikottai			2			1	3
6.	Karakkottai			1				1
7.	Keelamanjakkudi			1				1
8.	Kottaippattinam			10				10
9.	Manalur			2			1	3
10.	Minnamozhi			1				1
11.	Nerkuppam						1	1
12.	Nilayur	1						1
13.	Perumaruthur						1	1
14.	Vitchur						1	1
	Total	5		22			7	34

Source : Records, DRDA, Padukkottai District.

Table 2.29 : Village Panchayatwise details of the allocation of IAY Houses of Thiruvarankulam Union 2003–2004

Sl. No.	Name of the Panchayat	Categories						
		Freed bonded labour	Affected by riot	Widows	Fire Victims	Ex-service men	PH	Total
1.	Dakshinapuram	7		1				8
2.	Kalangudi			3			1	4
3.	Kathakurichi			5				5
4.	Kovilur			1		1	2	4
5.	Kulamanglam Therku			2				2
6.	Kuppakkudi						1	1
7.	L.N. Puram			1	2			3
8.	Mangadu				1			1
9.	Maniyambalam			1				1
10.	Manjanviduthi						2	2
11.	Nagaram						1	1
12.	Neduvasal West			1			1	2
13.	Palaiyur				1		2	3
14.	Pallathividuthi			3			1	4
15.	Panagulam						1	1
16.	Patchikkottai			1			1	2
17.	Pathampatti						2	2
18.	Pudukkottaividuthi			5				5
19.	Senthankudi						2	2
20.	Vennavalkudi			2			1	3
	Total	7		26	4	1	18	56

Source: Records, DRDA, Pudukkottai District.

WOMEN'S SANITARY COMPLEX

Women's sanitary complexes run independently by user groups of village women have become profitable ventures in Pudukkottai District after being dovetailed with the Total Rural Sanitation Programme, also being implemented in the district. One of the need based programmes of Tamil Nadu is the Integrated Sanitary Complex for Women and Children which has been well received by the people. Lack of privacy and dignity to rural women is slowly getting resolved and state of the art facilities are being set up across the state with plentiful water. Facilities for washing and bathing are a boon to the disadvantaged women. Being exclusive to women and with conveniences like electricity supply and lights the Women's Sanitary Complexes (WSCs) also give enough protection and privacy to the women users during day and night.

Box 13: Women's Sanitary Complex - A Success Story

The Women's Sanitary Complex located in Vathanakkottai Village Panchayat of Kunnandarkoil Block was constructed under a pilot scheme and now it is in proper use. The location of the complex is at the centre of the village. It is surrounded by many houses and a primary school. 100 members have associated themselves into the user group and are maintaining it neatly and they have got a matching grant of Rs.10,000 from the District Rural Development Agency. Being exclusive to women and with conveniences like electricity supply and lights it gives enough protection and privacy to the women during day and night. The caretaker's house is located near the Women's Sanitary Complex. So she can take proper care and she can give the key even at late night to the users without any inconvenience. All the inmates of the houses located around the complex have become members of the user group and they are paying Rs.5 each per month. This amount will be useful to pay the caretaker and to defray the maintenance charges.

These units managed by the women's user groups also help in empowering women and enabling them to make collective decisions. Demands for setting up WSCs in other villages are now pouring in.

In Pudukkottai District the utmost importance is being given to the scheme and the District Collector and the Project Officer, District Rural Development Agency, take personal interest in its implementation. The Integrated Sanitary Complex for Women and

Children (ISCWC) has thus become one of the most successful and need based programmes in the district. Since Pudukkottai District is also selected for the implementation of the Total Rural Sanitation Programme (TRSP) it has become possible to dovetail the programmes to mutual advantage and the district is bound to benefit immensely in the long run. A major training programme and constant monitoring have supplemented the schemes. The user groups (UGs) of WSCs are able to get a corpus fund, working capital for maintenance, caretaker wages, electricity bills etc. from the TRSP funds with an equal share collected from the users. This amount, which comes to Rs.20,000 is also available to the UG members for credit needs at a nominal interest. Thus, through professional management and dovetailing of programmes, the WSC programme has become very effective in Pudukkottai District.

Since the WSC units are managed by village women's collectives these are also independent of the government and they have evolved as a sustainable community resource. The UG consists of 100 members and, with their routine meetings and training inputs, they have become powerful in the rural areas. They place several demands before the Village Panchayat which has to take-care of them as they are a force to reckon with in many areas. Of the targeted 249 WSCs (2001-2002) in Pudukkottai District 109 have been physically completed and 71 handed over to the UGs while 53 WSCs have received the matching grant of Rs.10,000 and now have a total of Rs.20,000 with them, together with their own contribution. They are now able to lend to members at low interest and pay the electricity bills of the complex. In a few places, the Village Panchayats pay the monthly electricity bills of the WSCs and some of them find it a new burden. In Pudukkkottai District the monthly electricity bills as well as the wages of the caretaker, apart from the cost of minor repairs, are paid for by the UG. This is paid from the small monthly user fee of Rs.5 or Rs.10 as determined by the UG in various places. One of them gets a steady employment and income and some of these get Rs.500 per month which is a good amount in these areas. After meeting the expenses some of the groups also make a small profit which adds to their corpus fund.

A total of 31,520 members are enrolled as members of the UGs. They have all been put through intensive training. Capacity building for the members is a major input in Pudukkottai District and a lot of importance has been given to this. An inbuilt system of monitoring has been incorporated, with monitoring officers, district and block level committees and weekly progress reports among others put into operation.

Box 14

Weekly progress reports of the Women's Sanitary Complexes were collected to monitor the maintenance and usage by the Mukkiya Sevika of the Panchayat Union. The following table shows the progress report of the Women's Sanitary Complex of Parambur Gram Panchayat, Annavasal Block.

1.	Name of the location of the WSC	Parambur
2.	Name of the Village Panchayat	Parambur
3.	Date on which the complex was handed to the user group	6.10.2002
4.	Total members in the user group	50
5.	Did they get matching grant? If yes, how much?	Yes Rs. 10,000

6. Usage :

	Total Number	User Group		Non-user Group		Total Users
		Women	Children	Women	Children	
Toilet	8	40	10	-	-	50
Bathroom	3	50	-	-	-	50
Washing Stone	2	50	-	-	-	50

7.	Time of Usage	6 a.m. to 6 p.m.
8.	Appointment of caretaker	Yes
9.	Monthly salary for the caretaker	Rs.300
10.	Any problem in the usage and maintenance of the complex	Water usage is not streamlined

11.	Details of the presence of toilets in houses of members of user group : 1. Number of members who have toilet 2. Number of members who don't have toilet	 30 20
12.	Meeting of user group	Monthly
13.	Number of members who attend the meeting	30
14.	Presence of garden around the complex	Yes, planted plantain, sapota, tomato, coconut trees etc.
15.	Total amount under revolving fund among the user group	Rs.18,000
16.	Did any member borrow money from the user group to construct toilet. If yes, how many?	No
17.	Did the borrowers pay back the money with interest promptly? (other purpose)	Yes
18.	Total collection of monthly interest at present	Rs. 540
19.	Rate of monthly subscription from the users	Nil
20.	Charge for the use of complex by non-user group	Nil
21.	Electricity bill	Rs.633
22.	Miscellaneous	Rs.100
23.	Whether the user group has taken any measure to construct toilets for each house?	Yes
24.	If yes, did they receive any application for toilet construction?	Yes, 80
25.	How many have constructed toilets because of the user group's initiation?	20
26.	Any other matter to mention regarding WSC	Nil

Source: Records, Panchayat Union Office, Annavasal

This format will be filled by the Secretary of the user group with the help of the Mukkiya Sevika and the President of the user group will countersign it.

Quantum

Integrated Sanitary Complexes for Women and Children (ISCWCs) have been constructed in all the thirteen blocks of Pudukkottai District. The blockwise details of the availability of ISCWC in the year 2001-2002 are given hereunder:

Table 2. 30 : Village Panchayatwise details of the provision of ISCWC in Annavasal Union 2001-2002

Sl. No.	Name of the Panchayat	Name of the Hamlet
1.	Vayalokam	Vayalokam
2.	Kothirapatti	Malaikudipatti
3.	Narthamalai	Narthamalai
4.	Panampatti	Panampatti
5.	Parambur	Parambur
6.	Vellanur	Vellanur
7.	Vellanjar	Vellanjar
8.	Katharvampatti	Kathavampatti
9.	Killikudi	Killikudi
10.	Chithannavasal	Chithannavasal
11.	Thatchampatti	Thatchampatti
12.	Ennai	Meiyakavudampatti
13.	Mangudi	Mangudi
14.	Kothandaramapuram	Murugarajnagar
15.	Sathyamangalam	Alangulam
16.	Irundirapatti	Irundirapatti
17.	Perumanadu	Perumanadu
18.	Ariyur	Algapuri
19.	Pulvayal	Pulvayal .
20.	Thodaiyur	Thodaiyur
22.	Ammachatram	Ammachatram
	Total	22

Source: Records DRDA, Pudukkottai District

Table 2.31 : Village Panchayatwise details of the provision of ISCWC in Arimalam Union 2001-2002

Sl. No.	Name of the Panchayat	Name of the Hamlet
1.	Kaikulanvayal	K. Pudupatti
2.	Onankudi	Onankudi
3.	Karamangalam	Thenipatti
4.	Melnilaivayal	Melnilaipatti
5.	Embal	Embal
6.	Pilivayal	Pilivayal
7.	K.Rayavaram	K.Rayavaram
8.	Kadiyapatti	Kadiyapatti
9.	Thekkathur	Namanasamudram
10.	Punilaivayal	Keelanilaikottai
11.	Nedungudi	Kailasapuram
12.	Samudram	Tanjore
13.	Keelpanaiyur	Keelpanaiyur
14.	Rayavaram	Vasukipuram
15.	Valaramanickam	Valaramanickam
16.	Kummakudi	Thalampatti
	Total	16

Source: Records DRDA, Pudukkottai District

Table 2.32 : Village Panchayatwise details of the provision of ISCWC in Kunnandarkoil Union 2001-2002

Sl. No.	Name of the Panchayat	Name of the Hamlet
1.	Perambur	Perambur
2.	Uppiliyakudi	Uppiliyakudi
3.	Puliyur	Puliyur
4.	Vathanakottai	Vathanakottai
5.	Andankulam	Andankulam
6.	Killukottai	Killukottai
7.	Sengur	Melapatti
8.	Themmavur	Themmavur
9.	Killanur	Killanur
10.	Vaithur	Vaithur
11.	Vathanakurichi	Thirumalaiyapuram
12.	Veerakudi	Veerakudi
13.	T.Keelaiyur	Kulavaipatti
14.	Oliamangalam	Oliamangalam
15.	Odukkur	Odukkur
16.	Kulathur	Kulathur
17.	Nanjur	Nanjur
18.	Odugampatti	Odugampatti
19.	Udaiyalipatti	Udaiyalipatti
	Total	19

Source : Records DRDA, Pudukkottai District.

Table 2.33 : Village Panchayatwise details of the provision of ISCWC in Ponnamaravathi Union 2001-2002

Sl. No.	Name of the Panchayat	Name of the Hamlet
1.	Maravamadurai	Sadayampatti
2.	Alavayal	Alavayal
3.	Koppanapatti	Koppanapatti
4.	Thirukalampur	Thirukalampur
5.	Idaiyathur	Idaiyathur
6.	Oliyamangalam	Vellaiyapatti
7.	Melathaniyam	Melathaniyam
8.	Velakurichi	Velakurichi
9.	Nallur	Nallur
10.	Melasivapuri	Melasivapuri
11.	Varpattu	Varpattu
12.	Ammankurichi	Ammankurichi
13.	Vendanpatti	Vendanpatti
14.	Thottiyampatti	Periyarnagar
15.	Sempoothi	Sempoothi
16.	M.Usilampatti	M.Usilampatti
17.	Melamelnilai	Melamelnilai
18.	Sundaram	Sundaram
19.	Nagarapatti	Ammapatti
20.	Karaiyur	Karaiyur
21.	Nerunjikudi	Vellukudi
	Total	21

Source: Records DRDA, Pudukkottai District.

Table 2.34 : Village Panchayatwise details of the Provision of ISCWC in Viralimalai Union 2001-2002

Sl. No.	Name of the Panchayat	Name of the Hamlet
1.	Viralimalai	Viralimalai
2.	S.Nangudi	Mangudi
3.	Mathur	Mathur
4.	Kodumbalur	Kodumbalur
5.	Kalamavur	Kalamavur
6.	Thennathirayanpatti	Thennathirayanpatti
8.	Perambur	Melampatti
9.	Kumaramangalam	Nanjilarnagar
10.	Mandaiyur	Mandaiyur
11.	Vanthirayanpatti	Vanthirayanpatti
12.	Avoor	Avoor
13.	Suriyur	Eluvampatti
14.	Meenaveli	Chithirampatti
15.	Poiyamani	Sevalpattu
16.	Rajalipatti	Rajalipatti
17.	Buthakudi	Puruvai
18.	Thennampadi	Thennampadi
19.	Rajagiri	Rajagiri
20.	Thengaithinnipatti	Thengaithinnipatti
21.	Vilaipatti	Vilaipatti
22.	Virudapatti	Seralapatti
	Total	22

Source: Records DRDA, Pudukkottai District.

Table 2. 35 : Village Panchayatwise details of the provision of ISCWC in Thirumayam Union 2001-2002

Sl. No.	Name of the Panchayat	Name of the Hamlet
1.	Neyvasal	Sanmuganathapuram
2.	Thulaiyanur	Melaikudipatti
3.	Konapattu	Konapattu
4.	Melur	Melur
5.	Aranginampatti	Aranginampatti
6.	Kannur	Kannur
7.	Neykonnam	Neykonnam
8.	Kulipirai	Kulipirai
9.	Kulamangalam	Kulamangalam
10.	Kottur	Kottur
11.	Illanjavur	Illanjavur
12.	Lembakudi	Lembakudi
13.	Melapanaiyur	Purakaraipatti
14.	Virachilai	Virachilai
15.	Rangiyam	Rangiyam
16.	Vengalore	Vengalore
17.	V.Lakshmipuram	V.Lakshmipuram
	Total	17

Source: Records DRDA, Pudukkottai District.

Table 2.36 : Village Panchayatwise details of the provision of ISCWC in Pudukkottai Union 2001-2002

Sl. No.	Name of the Panchayat	Name of the Hamlet
1.	Perungalur	Perungalur
2.	Athankottai	Athanakottai
3.	Varapur	Nerujipatti
4.	Pudukkottai	Pudukkottai Bus Stand
5.	Thirumalairayasamudram	Thirumalaiyarayasamudram
6.	Pudukkottai	Pudukkottai South
7.	Muthur	Thenthiraiyanpatti
8.	Sempattur	Sempattur
9.	M.Kulavaipatti	Kulavaipatti
10.	Perunkodanviduthi	Kulaiyanviduthi
11.	Kavinadu	Sirunangupatti
12.	Kuppaiynapatti	Kuppaiyanpatti
13.	Puthambur	Puthambur
14.	Vadavalam	Vadavalam
15.	Sammattividuthi	Melaviduthi
	Total	15

Source: Records DRDA, Pudukkottai District.

Table 2.37 : Village Panchayatwise details of the provision of ISCWC in Aranthangi Union 2001-2002

Sl. No.	Name of the Panchayat	Name of the Hamlet
1.	Maramadaki	Maramadaki
2.	Nagudi	Nagudi
3.	Periyalur	V.S.K.Nagar
4.	Ayiggudi	Ayiggudi
5.	Cilatur	Cilatur
6.	Vembangudi East	Vembangudi East
7.	Ramasamypuram	Ramasamypuram
8.	Merpaniakadu	Merpanaikadu
9.	Neivathali	Neivathali
10.	Arasarkulam Keelpatti	Arasarkulam Keelpatti
11.	Poovarkudi	Poovarkudi
12.	Rathinakottai	Rathinakottai
13.	Alappiranthan	Nayakkarpatti
14.	Arasarkulam Thenpatti	Manickamkudiyiruppu
15.	Perunkadu	Perunkadu
16.	Thanthani	Thanthani
17.	Mangudi	Mangudi
18.	Arasarkulam Vadapatti	Arasarkulam Vadapatti
19.	Avanathankottai	Avanathankottai
20.	Aliyanilai	Aliyanilai
21.	Amanji	Duraiyarasapuram
22.	Vettivayal	Thittakudi
23.	Rajendrapuram	Rajendrapuram
24.	Melapattu	Melapattu
25.	Ekaperumalur	Thiruvangore
26.	Ekanivayal	Ekanivayal
	Total	26

Source: Records DRDA, Pudukkottai District.

Table 2.38 : Village Panchayatwise details of the provision of ISCWC in Avudayarkoil Union 2001-2002

Sl. No.	Name of the Panchayat	Name of the Hamlet
1.	Karur	Karur
2.	Pandipathiram	Pandipathiram
3.	Vettanur	Vettanur
4.	Meemisal	Meemisal
5.	Nattanipurasakudi	Gopalpattinam Meenavar Colony
6.	Velvarai	Velvarai
7.	Thiruperunthurai	Kulathukudiyiruppu
8.	Punniyavasal	Punniyavasal
9.	Keelacheri	Koduvayal
10.	Veeramangalam	Veeramangalam
11.	Thondaimanenthal	Karaniethal
12.	Poovalur	Piranthani
13.	Sirumaruthur	Vadamaruthur
14.	Kalabam	Kalabam
15.	Perumaruthur	Perumaruthur
16.	Kelkudivalathur	Kelkudi
17.	Ookur	Ookur
	Total	17

Source: Records DRDA, Pudukkottai District.

Table 2.39 : Village Panchayatwise details of the provision of ISCWC in Manamelkudi Union 2001-2002

Sl. No.	Name of the Panchayat	Name of the Hamlet
1.	Manamelkudi	Pathakadu
2.	Keelmanjakudi	Jegathapattinam
3.	Ammapattinam	Ammapattinam Meenavar Colony
4.	Kottapattinam	Kottaipattinam Colony
5.	Kattumavadi	Alavayal
6.	Nerkuppai	Ambalavanenthal
7.	Idaiyathimangalam	Idaiyathimangalam
8.	Karakottai	Singavanam
9.	Krishnajipattianam	Krishnajipattinam Meenavar Colony
10.	Mumbalai	Melasthanam Colony
11.	Manamelkudi	Ammapattinam North
12.	Ammapatinam	Ammapattinam South street
13.	Keelmanjakudi	Sellanenthal
	Total	13

Source: Records DRDA, Pudukkottai District.

Table 2.40 : Village Panchayatwise details of the provision of ISCWC in Gandarvakottai Union 2001-2002

Sl. No.	Name of the Panchayat	Name of the Hamlet
1.	Gandarvakottai	Gandarvakottai
2.	Gandarvakottai	Kothagam
3.	Manganore	Manganore
4.	Pudunagar	Pudunagar
5.	Pdupatti	Pudupatti
6.	Andanore	Manjampatti
7.	Periyakottai	Mokanore
8.	Pallavarayanpatti	Namburanpatti
9.	Gomapuram	Gomapuram
10.	Namburampatti	Namburanpatti
11.	Vellalaviduthi	Mangalakool
12.	Kallakottai	Kallakottai
13.	Palaiyugandarvakottai	Palyagandarvakottai
14.	Majapettai	Majapettai
15.	Ariyanipatti	Ariyanipatti
16.	Punakulam	Punakulam
17.	Mattangal	Mattangal
18.	Kurumpundi	Kurumpundi
	Total	18

Source: Records DRDA, Pudukkottai District.

Table 2.41 : Village Panchayatwise details of the provision of ISCWC in Karambakudi Union 2001-2002

Sl. No.	Name of the Panchayat	Name of the Hamlet
1.	Ambukoil	Ambukoil
2.	Vettanviduthi	Vettanviduthi
3.	Pilaviduthi	Pilaviduthi
4.	Thuthanviduthi	Uranipuram
5.	Kaliyaranviduthi	Kaliyaranviduthi
6.	Thirumanajeri	Thirumanajeri
7.	Pallavarayanpettai	Pudupatti
8.	Kalabam	S.Kalabam
9.	Malaiyur	Malaiyur
10.	Mankottai	M.Keelapatti
11.	Mudalipatti	Keelankadu
12.	Odappaviduthi	Manamadai A.D.Colony
13.	Pappapatti	Pappapatti
14.	Pannanviduthi	Pannanviduthi South
15.	Puduviduthi	Puduviduthi
16.	Sengamedu	Pathuthakku
17.	Keerathur	Thattamanaipatti
18.	Regunathapuram	Regunathapuram
19.	Mulankurichi	Mulankurichi
	Total	19

Source: Records, DRDA Pudukkottai District.

Table 2.42 : Village Panchayat wise details of the provision of ISCWC in Thiruvarankulam Union 2001-2002

Sl. No.	Name of the Panchayat	Name of the Hamlet
1.	Thiruvarankulam	Thiruvarankulam
2.	Vepakudi	Porpinakottaikoil
3.	Kayampatti	Kayampatti
4.	Vallathirakottai	Vallathirakottai
5.	Neduvasal East	Neduvasal East
6.	Kothamangalam	Kothamangalam
7.	Poovarasakudi	Alagambalpuram
8.	Melathur	Melathur
9.	Vennavalkudi	Vennavalkudi
10.	Pachikottai	AD Colony
11.	Kothakottai	Kothakottai
12.	Kulathur	Kulathur
13.	Kaikurichi	Vijayaregunathapuram
14.	Kallangudi	Kalibullanagar AD Colony
15.	Pudukkottaividuthi	Arasampatti
16.	Thirukattalai	Thirukattalai
17.	Vadakadu	Vadakadu
18.	Pullanviduthi	Melapullanviduthi
19.	Kulamangalam South	Kulamangalam South
20.	Araiyapatti	Araiyapatti
21.	Mankadu	Mankadu
22.	Kulamangalam North	Kulamangalam North
23.	Kovilur	Maikelpatti
24.	Sethangudi	Sethangudi
	Total	24

Source: Records, DRDA Pudukkottai District.

Innovations

In an interesting development some of the Women's Sanitary Complexes in Pudukkottai District have become profitable ventures through the device of user groups. An effective programme of the Government of Tamil Nadu, the Integrated Sanitary Complexes for Women and Children, has thus become very successful in most locations in Pudukkottai District. In the district the user groups running the WSCs function as SHGs and are now meeting all the costs from their own purse. This is contrary to the normal system of the Panchayats paying the WSCs' electricity bills in many places, thereby creating an additional burden for the small Panchayats.

The 100 members of the strong user groups deposit Rs.100 each, thereby collecting Rs.10,000, which is supported by a matching grant from the District Rural Development Agency. This amount is circulated for internal credit needs by the WSC user group, earning an interest. This is supplemented by the nominal monthly user fee of Rs.5 or Rs.10 per member as decided upon in the group, and the user group thus becomes able to pay the electricity bills and meet the routine maintenance costs. In many places they also pay wages to one member as a caretaker. In some cases these user groups have also been converted into Water and Sanitation Committees and the user group members are now motivating the villagers to have individual toilets under the Total Rural Sanitation Programme and earning a small income in the process by routing the incentives available under that programme.

One hundred members in the user groups, through their periodical meetings and interactions, have come to the public space. As they contribute and manage the complex, they develop certain capabilities and, as a result, they put forth demands to and exert pressure on the Gram Panchayats. Some of the women have developed leadership qualities. Wherever they are organized, they are powerful.

Impact

Administration in the twenty-first century should gear itself to ensure human development, economy, performance orientation, empowerment of the people, advocacy, technocracy, cultural specificity and women oriented structures and should have the lofty objective of human rights. Governmental departments, while preparing guidelines for schemes for the people, have started following these principles mentioned above.

The Women's Sanitary Complex is one such programme which is creating the following impact on society:

(1) The principle of collective ownership was introduced among the users of the Women's Sanitary Complex.
(2) Public enterprise has become user pay enterprise so that the maintenance can be proper and a cost effective principle can be adopted.
(3) Responsibility and accountability for maintaining the complex was entrusted to the women which made them the stakeholders of the project.
(4) Privacy, protection and dignity of rural women was restored.
(5) Sense of owning of public property and responsibility for its maintenance was inculcated in the minds of the people.
(6) The user group also gets to play a role in the motivation component of the Total Rural Sanitation Programme.
(7) Economically women will be benefited much through the matching grant and this may motivate them to save for the future.
(8) On the sanitation front, the concept of baby toilet inculcates the toilet culture from childhood onwards.

The present campaign on the sanitation front will reap rich rewards in health and sanitation in Pudukkottai District in the coming days. If the WSCs can be profitable there is also a possibility that there can be a large number of WSCs in the district if the initial investments are made available. Thus the Pudukkottai experiment can serve as a model for areas where the problem of sanitation exists. Together with the WSCs promotion of individual toilets has also caught the attention of the district administration and steady progress is being made in this area also.

Achievements

The programme of construction of Integrated Sanitary Complexes for Women and Children is being implemented well in Pudukkottai District. During 2001-2002, on a pilot basis, one complex per block was constructed in all the 13 blocks and all the complexes have been put to use. For using and maintaining the complexes, user groups exclusively for the sanitary complexes were formed by mobilizing the available SHGs and other women living in the vicinity where the sanitary complexes were located.

Now, under the second phase to cover 50 per cent of the Panchayats in the district, construction work is in progress with a revised design suitable to the district. This programme is a mega programme and aims at covering all the Panchayats in this district in two years. Probably this is the first time that, after completion of the work, the assets have been handed over to the user groups/ SHGs. Realizing the importance of the programme and to make it a complete success the DRDA has arranged a series of measures. In the first and pilot phase sufficient funds were not provided for provision of water supply to the complexes. In sedimentary areas at least Rs.1 lakh is required for a separate borewell, motor, energization etc. Moreover there is a feeling among the users that the number of toilets may be reduced. Hence a new design has been adopted keeping in view the demand and the availability of funds and ensuring adequate water supply. In the new design it is proposed to provide tiles in all the rooms, cut stones for flooring in the washing area, space for accommodating the caretaker, space for safe custody of cleaning equipments etc. apart from separate water supply and one toilet room exclusively for babies with a one-foot opening in the middle of the door. Under the pilot phase 13 sanitary complexes were constructed in all the blocks and handed over to the user groups and put to use. In many of the complexes kitchen garden had been created and they provide income to the SHGs and it is being used for maintenance of the complexes. A sum of Rs.26 lakhs was incurred as expenditure. Under phase two sanitary complexes have been proposed to be constructed in 50 per cent of the total Village Panchayats. Totally 249 complexes have been taken up in the Village Panchayats at an estimated cost of Rs.2 lakhs per complex. These complexes will be handed over to the user groups for use and maintenance in due course.

Salient Features

The salient features of the Women's Sanitary Complexes are:

(1) The entrepreneurial role of public organizations with a market based public administration resulting in efficiency and economy in the functioning can be witnessed in the use of the Women's Sanitary Complexes. For every sanitary complex user groups are being formed by mobilizing the available SHG members and other women living in the vicinity of the complex. NGOs, officials of government departments, various formal and informal groups available in the villages are also involved apart from Panchayat Presidents and other PRIs to motivate people to form user groups. To motivate the women to join user groups and to involve them actively in the programme it is proposed that if any woman joins the user group as its member by remitting an entry fee of Rs.100 a matching grant equal to the amount (maximum of Rs.10,000 to each user group) will be given to the group by the DRDA by converging other schemes such as IEC grant from Government of India for sanitation, DPAP, CNP, CWP etc. This has really motivated the women and in almost all villages where complexes are built women have overwhelmingly responded. Table 2.43 shows the use of Women's Sanitary Complexes in Annavasal Block:

Table 2. 43 : Utility of the Sanitary Complexes

Sr. No.	Name of the Panchayat	Total Members of user group	Total Entry Fees	Maching grant	Appointment of caretaker	Users				
						Women			Children	
						Toilet	Washing	Bathing	Toilet	Bathing
1.	Panampatti	100	10,000	-	Yes	20	20	20	10	10
2.	Parambur	100	10,000	10,000	Yes	50	50	50	20	20
3.	Malaikudipatti	80	10,000	-	Yes	20	20	20	10	10
4.	Vayalaogam	100	10,000	10,000	Yes	20	20	20	10	10
5.	Iruthirapatti	61	10,000	10,000	Yes	25	25	30	25	25
6.	Pulvayal	80	10,000	10,000	Yes	20	20	20	10	10
7.	Vellanchar	60	10,000	10,000	Yes	40	40	40	15	10
8.	Ariyur	60	10,000	10,000	Yes	45	45	45	15	17
9.	Kathavampatti	60	10,000	10,000	Yes	30	30	30	10	15
10.	Gothandarampuram	50	10,000	10,000	Yes	30	30	30	10	15
11.	Killikudi	80	10,000	10,000	Yes	30	30	30	10	15
12.	Mangudi	70	10,000	10,000	Yes	25	25	25	10	15

Source : Records Panchayat Union, Annavasal Union

(2) Training has been designed at several levels--one each for block level officers, zonal level officers and village level officers. Another training at the district level to sensitize all RD/DRDA/MT officials was conducted. NGOs, Panchayat Presidents, user group leaders and SHG leaders were involved in full strength at different levels to prove that the administration is really serious about implementing the scheme. In order to bring about awareness among the user groups and to provide a rough idea of the scheme and the component of sanitation, two booklets, one "user group bylaw", the other "users' reference guide" were printed and distributed. Apart from above, the pamphlets under the RCH programmes highlighting the importance of health and hygiene were printed and distributed. These booklets were distributed to all District/ Block/Panchayat level officials, NGOs, user group leaders, SHG leaders, Pudugai Puvaiyar Mandrams, Panchayat Presidents etc.

In addition to the above, two cultural teams were formed and training was given to the teams in spreading the sanitation message through art forms such as street plays, songs, dramas etc. These cultural teams have conducted cultural programmes at the village level. The expenditure in this regard has been proposed to be met from DPAP/INDP/CNP/CWP/RCH and other funds available with the district administration.

(3) To make the programme sustainable the following steps are envisaged:

-- Self Help concept is inbuilt into the user group (savings, credit, regular meetings etc.)

-- System of matching grant enables the group to generate income to maintain the complex by rotating the amount among themselves.

-- It is proposed to implement the Total Rural Sanitation Programme through the user groups and it is also proposed to give an incentive of Rs.50 for every household toilet put up in their area.

(4) Collection of user charges from non-members of user group helps to maintain the sanitary complex tidy and also wages can be given to the sweepers.

In many complexes a separate account is maintained and some complexes are running at profit and the user groups have made it a business.

Box 15: Earnings from Non-Member Users

Viralimalai Panchayat of Viralimalai Block has started and is running a complex as a business enterprise. A temple is located near the complex. On Tuesdays and Fridays a lot of devotees visit the temple regularly even from far away places and they use the sanitary complex by paying Re.1 each. Through this they collect more than Rs.100 per day during these days. The caretaker is paid well and the maintenance is neat. Another complex in Maramadaki Panchayat of Aranthangi Block also collects Re.1 from non-members. The Monday weekly market which is located behind the complex earns a good income. User-pay basis has created a drastic change in these areas economically and has also contributed to keeping the surroundings clean.

(5) Gardens around the sanitary complexes earn some income and keep the complexes eco-friendly.

(6) Acute water shortage in some areas has made the public use the sanitary complexes. Seeing this utility, men are also demanding the same for them.

Box 16: Bathing and Washing Facility in Demand

An important reason for the popularity of the Women's Sanitary Complex is its water facility. Acute water shortage has forced the womenfolk to make use of the complex which has a borewell facility. In Parambur Panchayat, Annavasal Block, non-member women come from far away places to wash the clothes of the family. They also bring the other women of their family to bathe so that they do not suffer because of water scarcity. The water from the borewell serves nearly 50 houses daily mainly for washing and bathing. Even women from minority communities are coming out of their homes to avail of the facilities of the Women's Sanitary Complex. Seeing this utility, men are also demanding the same for them.

Points for Consideration

In spite of the above mentioned features consideration has to be given to the following points:

(1) Women should be motivated to use the toilet. It is seen that the complexes are used for washing and bathing since they do not have water in their houses.

> **Box 17: Toilets Ignored**
>
> It is obvious, that a few of the women are using the complex only for washing and bathing and do not use the toilets. In Pathakadu hamlet of Manamelkudi, a pond was created near the complex. Earlier the women were using the pond for bathing and washing, ignoring the presence of the Women's Sanitary Complex. Since the pond has dried up now they are coming to the complex, that too only for washing and bathing and not to use the toilet. So even now the benefit of using toilets has not reached the womenfolk fully.

(2) User groups should be identified before the construction is started, because some of the complexes, even after completion, were not put to use immediately. But the administration has assured that hereafter construction will be started only after the formation of the user group. There is also a proposal to give the construction contract to the user group itself.

(3) There is unrestricted use of water because of the availability of washing and bathing facilities. The use of water has to be streamlined. If the use is not streamlined a heavy burden will fall on the shoulders of the user group as they have to pay a heavy amount in the form of electricity charges.

> **Box 18: High Electricity Charges**
>
> Due to the availability of good water facility women are using the complex without any restriction in many places. Most of the complexes are open for a long time because women wash clothes throughout the day for all their family members. So, the motor of the borewell is running all the time and this results in high electricity charges. The Secretary of the Maramadaki Panchayat Women's Sanitary Complex said that the cost of the electricity for the motor alone was more than Rs.800. Last time she paid Rs.850 for electricity. Even though they get more income by collecting from non- member users group, she feared that the borewell will dry up very soon. So, in the next meeting of the user group, they have decided to draw a framework for streamlining the water usage.

(4) While selecting the habitations, it should be ascertained that sufficient rural households are available and where SHGs are active.

Box 19: Lack of Foresight

In Ammapattinam Panchayat, a Muslim dominated area located in Manamelkudi Union, the Women's Sanitary Complex, even after completion, was not in proper use mainly because of the location. It is located near the seashore rather far away from the habitations. Women are using a pond for washing and bathing but not coming to the complex because they feel that it is located in a place which they think will not be safe for them. Similarly, in Vayalokam Panchayat of Annavasal Block, people were not consulted before the construction of the complex. The complex is now located near a temple and women are not keen to use it since they consider the place sacred. Further, before sinking borewell, a geo-survey was not conducted. There is no ground water in both the complexes at Ammapattinam and Vayalogam. So, these complexes have been abandoned and do not serve the needs of the women.

(5) Before execution a geo-survey has to be conducted to assess the availability of water. Some of the complexes are not functioning because there is no water in the borewell.

(6) Some constructions were put up in disputed land which has led to disputes among social groups in the rural areas and therefore the WSC cannot be put to proper use.

Box 20: Need for Foresight

In Vetanviduthi Panchayat of Karambakudi Union, while the sanitary complex was under construction, some problems came to the fore because of encroachments but they were solved legally. Even after that some culprits are creating some inconvenience for proper usage. Even though the Panchayat President assured of due use in the future these things should be considered before the construction.

SAMPOORNA GRAMEEN ROZGAR YOJANA (SGRY)

About the Scheme

Creation of employment opportunities with food security has been an important objective of developmental planning in India. The high growth of population and labour force has led to an increase in the volume of unemployment and underemployment from one Plan period to another. The Government of India aims at generating employment by offering manual work and self-employment with the goal of reducing unemployment and underemployment and of providing food security. Such an approach is necessary because it is realized that larger and efficient use of available human and other resources is the most effective way of alleviating poverty, reducing inequalities, improving nutritional levels and sustaining a reasonably high pace of economic growth.

To make a dent in the prevailing poverty, unemployment and slow growth in the rural economy and to provide food security it is necessary to provide a demand driven infrastructure at the village level to facilitate faster growth in the rural areas and to increase opportunities of employment through access to the market oriented economy.

To provide a thrust to additional wage employment, infrastructural development and food security in the rural areas, the Prime Minister of India announced on 15th August 2001 the launching of an ambitious new scheme with an annual outlay of Rs.10,000 crores. Accordingly the Ministry of Rural Development reviewed the hitherto ongoing schemes of the Employment Assurance Scheme (EAS) (the only additional wage employment scheme for rural areas), the Jawahar Gram Samridhi Yojana (JGSY) (a rural infrastructre development scheme) and, by merging them into one scheme, launched a new scheme known as the Sampoorna Gramin Rozgar Yojana (SGRY) w.e.f. 25th September 2001.

Objectives

The Sampoorna Grameen Rozgar Yojana (SGRY) will have the following objectives:

Primary Objective

The primary objective of the scheme is to provide additional wage employment in all rural areas and thereby provide food security and improve nutritional levels.

Secondary Objective

The secondary objective is the creation of durable community, social and economic assets and infrastructural development in rural areas.

Status

The programme will be implemented as a centrally sponsored scheme on cost sharing basis between the Centre and the States in the ratio of 75:25 of the cash component of the programme. In the case of UTs the Centre will provide the entire (100%) funds for the scheme. Foodgrains will be provided to the States/UTs free of cost.

Target Group

The SGRY will be open to all rural poor who are in need of wage employment and desire to do manual and unskilled work in and around their village/habitat. The programme is self-targeting in nature.

While providing wage employment, preference will be given to agricultural wage earners, non-agricultural unskilled wage earners, marginal farmers, women, members of Scheduled Castes and Scheduled Tribes, parents of child labourers liberated from hazardous occupations, parents of handicapped children and adult children of handicapped parents who are desirous of working for wage employment.

Programme Strategy

(1) Five per cent of the funds and the foodgrains under the SGRY will be retained in the Ministry for utilization in the areas of acute distress arising out of natural calamities or for taking up preventive measures in chronically drought or flood affected rural areas. Savings from the five per cent can be allotted by the Ministry to better performing districts.

(2) A certain percentage of the allotted foodgains under the SGRY will be reserved for the special component to be used in any Central or State Government scheme with wage employment potential to meet exigencies arising out of any natural calamity.

(3) The remaining funds and foodgrains under the SGRY will be available in two streams from the Department of Rural Development.

First Stream

The first stream will be implemented at the District and Intermediate Panchayat levels. Fifty per cent of the funds and foodgrains will be available under the first stream and will be distributed to the Zila Parishads and the Intermediate Panchayats in the ratio of 40:60.

Second Stream

The second stream will be implemented at the Village Panchayat level and 50 per cent of the funds and foodgrains will be earmarked for the Village Panchayats and distributed among them through DRDAs/zila Parishads.

(4) The programme will be implemented through the Panchayati Raj Institutions (PRIs).

Special Safeguards for the Weaker Sections and Women of the Community

— 22.5 per cent of the annual allocation (inclusive of foodgrains) under the first stream of the scheme shall be earmarked for individual beneficiary schemes of SC/ST families living below the poverty line (BPL).

— A minimum 50 per cent of the allocation to the Village Panchayat (inclusive of foodgrains) will be earmarked for the creation of need based village infrastructure in SC/ST habitations/Wards under the second stream of the SGRY.

— 30 per cent of employment opportunities shall be reserved for women.

Definition of Panchayats

(1) Village Panchayat in these guidelines means the lowest elected body and includes Gram Panchayats, Mandals, Nagar Panchayats or traditional village institutions like Village Councils and Village Development Boards having a statutory character.

(2) Where the duly elected Village Panchayat is not in existence, its sharc of funds will bc passed on to the Administrator/ Administrative Committee which will be responsible for implementing the second stream of the SGRY in such Panchayats. The works to be taken up will, however, be decided at the village level itself by the Gram Sabha (Village Assembly) of the concerned Panchayat.

(3) District and Intermediate Panchayats mean elected bodies at the District and the Block levels respectively and include similar traditional institutions having statutory character where the Panchayat Act is not applicable.

(4) Where the duly elected District or Intermediate Panchayat is not in existence, the DRDA at the District level and the Administration/Administrative Committee at the Block level will be responsible for implementing the first stream of the SGRY.

(5) Where the Panchayat Act is not applicable and traditional institutions also do not exist at the District and Block levels, the DRDA at the District level and a committee consisting of

the heads of the Village Councils etc. and chaired by the BDO at the Block level will be responsible for implementing the first stream of the SGRY.

(6) The forest villages which are not part of any existing Village Panchayat will be treated as Village Panchayats.

Foodgrains under SGRY

Foodgrains shall be given as part of wages under the SGRY. Distribution of foodgrains under the SGRY (first and second streams) is based on the principle of protecting the real wages of the workers besides improving the nutritional standards of the families of the rural poor. Foodgrains shall be given as part of wages under the SGRY to the rural poor at the rate of 5 kg per manday. Should a State Government wish to give more than 5 kg of foodgrains per manday, it may do so within the existing State allocation (subject to the condition that a minimum of 25 per cent of the wages is to be paid in cash). The State Governments and UT Administrations will be free to calculate the cost of foodgrains paid as part of wages at a uniform rate which may be either BPL rate or APL rate or anywhere between the two rates. The workers will be paid the balance of the wages in cash so that they are assured of a certain amount of cash per manday while the higher price fixed for the foodgrains will result in saving of the cash component which may be utilized to meet the material cost for creation of durable community assets.

The Central Government will provide foodgrains and cash component to the States and UT Administrations as per the criteria in order to generate additional wage employment. If there is a balance of foodgrains from the SGRY the same can be utilized for dovetailing with Central/State sector schemes provided 100 per cent cash requirement is available for such schemes. Distribution of foodgrains to the workers under the programme will be either through PDS or by the Gram Panchayat or any other agency appointed by the State Government. Distribution of foodgrains will be made to the workers most preferably at the work site. In the event of the workers belonging to one habitation choosing to receive the foodgrains in their habitation, the same can be organized. While the State Government will have the option of utilizing the PDS it will have to be ensured that effective safeguards are in place to avoid leakages. The DRDAs/ZPs will make necessary arrangements for distribution of foodgrains to the concerned agencies.

Distribution and Release of Foodgrains

The Department of Rural Development will intimate the quantity of foodgrains to be released to the State with the districtwise details. The Department of Food and Public Distribution will thereafter send an appropriate advice to the FCI under intimation to the Department of Rural Development and the Secretary (RD) of the State to release foodgrains from its designated depots to the authorized agencies of the State Governments/ZPs/DRDAs.

The Department of Rural Development will release funds for the foodgrains directly to the FCI which will be required to send bills duly verified by the DRDA/ZP to the Department of Rural Development on the basis of statements of quantities of foodgrains allocated and lifted districtwise, signed jointly by the PO (DRDA)/ Zila Parishad and the District Manager, FCI. At the district level the PO (DRDA)/ZP will coordinate the release and lifting of stocks under the programme. No payment will be required to be made to the FCI at the depots by the DRDA or the Authorized Agency for lifting foodgrains within the districtwise allocation communicated by the Ministry of Rural Development/Department of Food and Public Distribution.

Procedure for Lifting of Foodgrains from FCI Depots

DRDAs/ZPs will identify the nearest depot of the FCI from which they propose to lift the foodgrains so that there is economy in the transportation charges for lifting of foodgrains. The district office of the FCI will issue release authorization against the district allocation for the SGRY programme. It will be desirable if the ZPs/

DRDAs intimate the quantities of foodgrains likely to be lifted by them on a monthly or a quarterly basis. The FCI is obliged to issue the foodgrains available with it. However, advance intimation is likely to help in ensuring adequate stocks in the concerned depots. Lifting of SGRY foodgrains for all the implementing agencies including the Intermediate Panchayats and the Gram Panchayats will have to be made either by the ZPs/DRDAs themselves or through their authorized agencies only.

Stocks once issued will not be taken back by the FCI. It will, therefore, be the responsibility of the DRDAs/ZPs to check if the common rice supplied to them conforms to the Fair Average Quality (FAQ). The concerned officers of the DRDAs/ZPs should conduct inspection of the stocks before taking delivery of the same to ensure that foodgrains below the FAQ are not dumped on them. The normal procedure by way of joint sampling, as is done for the PDS, will operate. In case of any complaint, the sample from the field will be compared with the sample packet retained at the FCI depot and action will be initiated against all responsible in this behalf, if any discrepancy is established.

Provision of Transportation

The State Government/Union Territories will bear the transportation cost and other handling charges from their own resources. Any taxes/charges like sales tax, octroi etc. will be borne by the concerned States/UTs. The cash component of the SGRY cannot be used for transportation, payment of local taxes etc.

Disposal of Empty Gunny Bags

The gunny bags in which the foodgrains are received for distribution under the programme will be disposed of in accordance with the prescribed procedure in the State and the sale proceeds of the same can be used for making payment towards the transportation cost/ handling charges.

Wages Under SGRY

Wages under the programme shall be paid partly in foodgrains and partly in cash. The minimum wages fixed by the State authorities shall be paid under the SGRY both for skilled and unskilled labour. Equal wages shall be paid under the programme to both men and women workers. Payment of wages shall be made on a fixed day in a week, preferably a day before the local market day, in the presence of the Village Pradhan/Sarpanch/Panchas. In case the executive agencies do not pay the wages for a category of employment at the rate notified for the relevant schedule of employment under the Minimum Wages Act, the Zila Parishad/ Panchayat Samiti shall withhold further release of funds to that implementing agency and inform the fact to the concerned authority for suitable action against the erring officials under the Minimum Wages Act and also inform the Central Government. Where the Central Government finds that the above provisions are not being followed, it may withhold further release of funds under the programme to the concerned district.

Criteria, Allocation and Utilization of Resources

First Stream

Allocation of Funds/Foodgrains from Centre to State/UTs and the Districts

Under the scheme funds and foodgrains will be allocated to the States/UTs on the basis of proportion of the rural póor in a State to the total rural poor in the country or such other criteria as decided by the Central Government from time to time. At the district level the allocation of funds and foodgrains will be made on the index of backwardness formulated on the basis of the proportion of the rural SC/ST population in a district to the total SC/ST population in the State and inverse of per capita production of the agricultural workers in that district. Equal weightage will be give to these two criteria, while allocating funds and foodgrains to the district.

Distribution of Funds among Zila Parishads/DRDAs and Panchayat Samitis

Zila Parishads/DRDAs

Forty per cent of the funds and foodgrains earmarked under the first stream will be reserved at the district level and shall be utilized by the Zila Parishads/DRDAs preferably in the areas suffering from endemic labour exodus or areas of distress, as per the Annual Action Plan approved by the Zila Parishads/DRDAs.

Panchayat Samitis

Sixty per cent of the funds and foodgrains earmarked under the first stream will be allocated among the Panchayat Samitis (Intermediate Panchayats). While allocating the funds and foodgrains, equal weightage will be given to the proportion of SC/ST population and of rural population of the respective Panchayat Samiti areas to those of the Districts. The works will be taken up as per their own Annual Action Plan approved by the Panchayat Samitis. However, while selecting the work to be taken up, preference will be given to the areas which are backward, calamity prone or face migration of labour.

Earmarking and Utilization of Resources

There will be no sectoral earmarking of resources under the first stream of the SGRY except that 22.5 per cent of the annual allocation of the Zila Parishad/DRDA and of the Intermediate Panchayat must be spent on individual beneficiary schemes for SCs/STs below the poverty line. Diversion of funds meant for SCs/STs to other works is not permitted: 22.5 per cent of the resources released to the Zila Parishad and Intermediate level Panchayat shall be used for individual works for SCs/STs. The illustrative list of such economic assets/works which can be taken up for the benefit of identified individuals belonging to SCs/STs are as hereunder:

Development of allotted land in the case of allottees of ceiling surplus land, Bhoodan land, government land;

Social forestry works, such as fuel wood and fodder plantations on private lands belonging to SCs/STs;

Agri-horticulture, floriculture plantation on private lands belong to SCs/STs below poverty line;

Work shed or infrastructure for any self-employment programme;

Open irrigation wells/borewells for irrigation;

Pond excavation/re-excavation with primary support for pisciculture; and

Other sustainable income generation assets.

Second Stream

The second stream of the SGRY will be implemented at the Village Panchayat level for generation of supplementary wage employment and creation of demand driven community/village infrastructure which includes durable assets to enable the rural poor to increase opportunities for sustained employment. Out of the total resources earmarked under the SGRY, fifty per cent of the funds are earmarked for the second stream of the SGRY. The entire resources released under the second stream will be distributed among the Gram Panchayats directly by the DRDAs/Zila Parishads. While, during the current year (2001-02) the allocation and release of resources will continue as per the existing criteria for the JGSY, from the second financial year (2002-03) onwards, the allocation of funds will be made in such a manner that each Panchayat receives at least a certain minimum of resources as to be determined from year to year. The State and Districtwise allocations will be made by the Ministry of Rural Development at the Central level. At the

Panchayat level, the DRDAs/Zila Parishads will make the allocation to each Panchayat as per the criteria. The base year allocation will not get affected if there is subsequent increase or decrease in the number of Panchayats in each district. If there is increase in the number of Panchayats in any given year, the share of each Panchayat will be reduced proportionately. If there is decrease in the number of Panchayats, the share of each Panchayat will be increased proportionately.

A minimum fifty per cent of the allocation to the Village Panchayat (inclusive of foodgrains) shall be earmarked for the creation of need-based village infrastructure in SC/ST habitations/ Wards under the second stream of the SGRY. Village Panchayats are permitted to spend upto a maximum of fifteen per cent of the funds on maintenance of the public assets created under the wage employment programmes sponsored by the Ministry of Rural Development from time to time within their geographical boundary. Under the second stream of the SGRY, Village Panchayats may spend upto a maximum of 7.5 per cent of the annual allocation of funds or Rs.7,500, whichever is less, during a year on administration, contingencies and for technical consultancy.

Release of Central Assistance

Central Assistance from the Department of Rural Development will be released every year directly to the DRDAs/ZPs in two instalments, subject to the fulfilment of the following conditions:

(1) *First Instalment:* The districts which obtained the second instalment of funds and foodgrains in the preceding financial year without any condition shall automatically receive the first instalment under both the streams. Others shall have to submit the proposal for the 1st instalment with necessary documents or after fulfilling the conditions imposed while releasing the second instalment for the previous year.

(2) *Second Instalment:* The second instalment of Central assistance (inclusive of foodgrains) will be released on request from DRDAs/

ZPs separately under both the streams in the prescribed proforma and *mutadis mutandis* on fulfilment of the following conditions:

(a) Sixty per cent of the total available funds, that is, opening balance of the year plus the amount received including the State share and other receipts, should have been utilized at the time of submitting the proposal for the second instalment.

(b) Seventy-five per cent of the foodgrains allocated as first instalment should have been lifted and sixty per cent of the lifted foodgrains (including the balance) should have been utilized along with a reconciled statement of the quantity lifted to be signed by the PD/DRDA/CEO/Zila Parishad and FCI District Manager. The State government shall release its matching share to the DRDAs/ZPs within a fortnight of the release of the Central assistance (cash component). The funds and foodgrains to Intermediate Panchayats (under stream I) and resources to the Village Panchayats (under stream II) will be distributed by the DRDAs/ZPs within fifteen days from the Central or the State Government, as the case may be. Distribution of the Central share should not wait for the matching State share. In the case of forest villages the DRDAs/ZPs will place the allocated funds at the disposal of the respective district level forest officials. The forest authority of the district level will utilize these funds to take up works in the forest villages through a committee of five members consisting of at least one SC/ST woman and as per the felt needs of the village community in respect of works taken up by the Village Panchayats.

Ban on Contractors

The programme will be implemented only departmentally. Contractors are not permitted to be engaged for execution of any of the works under the programme. No middleman or any other intermediate agency should be employed for executing works under the programme. The full benefit of the wages to be paid should reach the workers and the cost of the works should not involve any commission charges payable to such contractors, middlemen, or intermediate agencies.

Muster Rolls

Muster rolls shall be maintained for every work separately showing the details of the wages paid to the workers and the foodgrains distributed. The muster rolls should show the number and the details of Scheduled Castes/Scheduled Tribes/ Women and others who have been provided employment. Those responsible for the preparation of the muster rolls should be responsible for these entries also. To prevent non-payment or under-payment of wages or any other manipulation, the muster rolls should be maintained in stitched form and all its pages must be numbered. Muster rolls shall be made available to the public on demand. For works taken up by the Village Panchayats under the SGRY, muster roll copies duly certified by the Panchayat Sarpanch shall be placed before every Gram Sabha.

Records of the Assets

Each District, Block and Village Panchayat shall maintain a complete inventory of the assets created under the programme, giving details of the date of the starting and the date of the completion of the project, cost involved, benefits obtained, employment generated and other relevant particulars. Information boards should be displayed near the works giving these details. A photographic record of the work may also be kept of the various stages of the implementation showing the status before starting, during implementation and after completion.

Audit

Both physical and financial audit of the works under the scheme are compulsory. This must be carried out at the end of the financial year by each district. This audit will be done either by the Local

Fund Auditors or by the Chartered Accountants listed in the panel of the State Governments or the AGs of the States or the C&AG. The audit report, together with action taken on the auditor's observations, shall be furnished at the time of applying for the second instalment of funds for the next financial year.

Social Audit

Immediately upon completion of works under the scheme the Zilla Parishads/ DRDAs shall publicize and inform the Gram Panchayats of the details of the works to ensure transparency, accountability and social control. The Gram Panchayats shall place these details before the respective Gram Sabhas. As regards Village Panchayats the meeting of the Gram Sabha shall be held every quarter on a fixed date and at a specified time and place to consider the issues regarding planning, execution, monitoring and supervision. These meetings shall be open to all members of the village community who shall be free to raise any issue regarding implementation of the scheme. The Gram Sabha shall also be kept informed of the progress of the implementation of the scheme and all other related issues.

Annual Action Plan

Each Zila Parishad/DRDA, Intermediate and Village Panchayat shall independently prepare and approve, before the beginning of each financial year, an Annual Action Plan equivalent in value to about 125 per cent of its share of funds allocated in the preceding year. No work can be taken up unless it forms part of the Annual Action Plan. The exercise of approval of the Annual Action Plan shall be completed by the end of February of the preceding financial year. To ensure meaningful utilization of resources under the SGRY routine division of resources among the Wards of the Gram Panchayat and among the constituencies of the Panchayat Samiti and of the Zila Parishad is prohibited. Works included in the Annual Action Plan should be need based and properly prioritized. Looking to the priorities of the works and the availability of resources only so many works shall be taken up as can be completed within a year and in exceptional circumstances in a maximum period of two years.

While preparing the Annual Action Plan, completion of the incomplete works including those of the EAS/JGSY should be given priority over the taking up of new works. No works shall be taken up which cannot be completed in one year or at the most within two financial years. As soon as the Annual Action Plan is finalized, the Zila Parishads/DRDAs and Intermediate Panchayats shall inform the concerned Gram Panchayats about the works selected for their areas. Works to be taken up by ZPs/DRDA and intermediate Panchayats shall be labour intensive. Works requiring larger component of materials like cement, steel etc. should not be sanctioned unless the excess cost on material component is provided from other sectoral programme funds. The Annual Action Plan prepared by the Village Panchayat shall be thoroughly discussed in the meeting of the Gram Sabha. Similarly the Annual Action Plan prepared by the ZPs/DRDAs and Intermediate Panchayats shall be thoroughly discussed in their respective general bodies. The Gram Sabha in respect of Village Panchayats and the general bodies in respect of ZPs/DRDAs and Intermediate Panchayats shall approve the Annual Action Plan and this shall be intimated to the Panchayat Samiti and ZPs/DRDAs. The administrative sanction for the works under the Annual Action Plan will be given by the competent authority as decided upon by the State/UT. The technical sanction will be accorded as per the rules of the State Government/ Union Territories.

The following works shall not be taken up under the SGRY:

(a) Building for religious purposes such as temple, mosque, gurudwara, church etc.

(b) Monuments, memorials, statutes, idols, arches/welcome gates.

(c) Bridges.

(d) Building for higher secondary schools.

(e) Building for colleges.

(f) Black topping of roads.

Works taken up under the scheme shall be of a durable nature and shall meet technical standards and specifications, if any, for the concerned work/area. Efforts shall be made to utilize local materials and cost effective technology developed by various institutions. The items of work approved by the Intermediate Panchayats for their share of funds in the manner prescribed above shall be charged to the Zila Parishads/DRDAs. In order to facilitate the technical scrutiny of the works, the officials of the Zila Parishads/DRDAs may prepare and approve standard designs and cost estimates of those items of works which are common in nature.

Works to be Taken Up Under Second Stream

All works that result in the creation of durable productive community assets can be taken up under the SGRY as per the felt needs of the area/people. Priority shall be given in the following order:

(a) Infrastructure support for Swarnajyanthi Gram Swarozgar Yoajana (SGSY).

(b) Infrastructure required for supporting agricultural activities in the Village Panchayat.

(c) Community infrastructure for education (including kitchen sheds), health and internal as well as link roads (roads linking the village to the main road, even if they fall outside the Panchayat area, are allowed to be constructed).

(d) Other socio-economic community assets.

(e) Desiltation, renovation of traditional village tanks/ponds.

Implementing Agencies of First Stream

The executing agencies of the first stream of the SGRY within a district can be any line department, corporation of the State Government, Panchayati Raj Institution (PRI) at all the three levels or well reputed NGOs approved by the Zila Parishads/DRDAs. It shall be the duty of the head of each executing agency in the district to scrupulously ensure the implementation of the works allotted by the Zila Parishads/DRDAs and Intermediate Panchayats. All executing agencies shall be responsible to the Zila Parishads / DRDAs / Panchayati Samitis for the proper maintenance of accounts of the expenditure incurred, measurement of physical work done, payment of wages to labour, submission of periodical statement of attendance, details of work and accounts for all works entrusted to them under the first stream of the SGRY.

Implementing Agencies for Second Stream

The scheme will be implemented through Village Panchayats, who will be responsible for planning and execution of the Yojana. The technical supervision will be the responsibility of the DRDAs/ZPs. Execution of works can be entrusted to well established self help groups. At the village level the entire work relating to coordination, review, supervision and monitoring of the programme will be the responsibility of the Village Panchayat. The Panchayats will execute the work. The Panchayat will have the power to execute works/ schemes upto Rs.1,00,000 with the approval of the Gram Sabha. No other administrative or technical approval will be necessary. Preparation of cost estimates for works/schemes upto Rs.1,00,000 will be the sole responsibility of the Gram Panchayats. But the Gram Panchayat should get the estimates of the works prepared by technically qualified people and check the measurements of work done with reference to estimates prior to payment. However for works/schemes costing more than Rs.1,00,000 after obtaining the approval of the Gram Sabha, the Gram Panchayat shall seek the technical/administrative approval of the appropriate authorities. In case of shortage of technical staff or otherwise it shall be permissible for the Village Panchayat to have the projects technically appraised by even private technically qualified people.

Quantum of Work

Table 2.44 : Quantum of work done under SGRY in 2002-03 in Pudukkottai District

Sl. No.	Work Name	Overall		
		Taken-up	Completed	Pending
1.	Bathing Ghat	16	13	3
2.	Bus Shelter	11	9	2
3.	Causeways	2	2	-
4.	Community Centre	1	-	1
5.	Culverts	209	198	11
6.	Desilting	9	8	1
7.	Drainage	34	34	-
8.	GH Reconstruction	16	15	1
9.	GH Repairs	729	719	10
10.	Group Houses	1	1	-
11.	IMP to Shandy	1	1	-
12.	Kitchen Shed	9	6	3
13.	Library Building	1	1	-
14.	MI Tank & Sluice	122	116	6
15.	Oorani	285	271	14
16.	Other Buildings	1	-	1
17.	Others	5	4	1
18.	PDS Outlet	2	1	1
19.	Plantation	14	14	-
20.	Repairs to kitchen	1	1	-
21.	Repairs to PT office	51	46	5
22.	Repairs to school	8	8	-
23.	Repairs (others)	95	82	13
24.	Repairs to Roads	2	1	1

Table 2.44 *(Contd.)*

Sl. No.	Work Name	Overall		
		Taken-up	Completed	Pending
25.	Retaining wall	28	26	2
26.	Road work - BT	3	-	3
27.	Road work - CC	71	70	1
28.	Road work - Gravel	82	69	13
29.	Road work - WBM	347	300	47
30.	SHG Building	198	21	177
31.	Shopping Complex	2	2	-
32.	Supply Channel	6	6	-
33.	Temple Tank	15	15	-
34.	Threshing Floor	285	263	22

Source: DRDA Records, Pudukkottai District.

Table 2.44 presents the abstract of the overall work (physical) for the year 2004. Among these thirty four works the predominant one was Government Hospital repairs, for which 729 works were taken up and 710 were successfully completed while the remaining 10 works are in progress. Road work (WBM) stands second, for which 347 works were taken up and 300 works have been successfully completed while the remaining 47 works are in progress. Oorani and threshing floor works occupy the third place in the total work allocation. For each of these 285 works were allotted. In the case of oorani maintenance 14 works are in progress while 271 works have been successfully completed. Except the SHG building work almost all the works have been completed. In the case of the SHG building, selection of site for the building takes much time compared to other works. SHG buildings are constructed by the beneficiaries themselves with the guidance of the Union engineers.

Quantum of Work Done Under SGRY

Stream I and Stream II

The abstract of the works (physical) carried out under the SGRY stream I for the year 2002-2003 is shown in Table 2.45.

Table 2.45 : Works carried out under SGRY

Sl. No.	Work Name	Overall		
		Taken-up	Completed	Pending
1.	Culverts	2	2	-
2.	Desilting	9	8	1
3.	Drainage	4	4	-
4.	GH Reconstruction	16	15	1
5.	GH Repairs	606	603	3
6.	Group Houses	1	1	-
7.	MI Tank & Sluice	100	95	5
8.	Oorani	204	196	8
9.	Others	1	-	1
10.	PDS Outlet	1	-	1
11.	Plantation	14	14	-
12.	Repairs	5	4	1
13.	Retaining Wall	3	2	1
14.	Road Work - BT	1	-	1
15.	Road Work - Gravel	2	-	1
16.	Road Work - WBM	44	29	15
17.	SHG Building	179	18	161
18.	Temple Tank	15	15	-

Source: DRDA Records, Pudukkottai District.

Under stream I of the SGRY, eighteen items of work were carried out in Pudukkottai District in the year 2002-2003. The first priority among all these works was to the work of GH repairs, for which 606 works were allotted, of which 603 works have been successfully completed in all the thirteen blocks in Pudukkottai District. Under the first stream the next priority was given to oorani maintenance, for which 204 works were taken up, of which 196 have been completed. For SHG buildings 179 works were taken up, of which 18 works have been completed and the remaining 161 works are in progress. Most of the other works have been successfully completed with just one or two pending. Culverts, desilting, drainage, GH reconstruction, group houses, PDS outlet, plantation, repairs, retaining wall, road work (BT), road work (gravel), temple tank maintenance have been carried out with one or two terms of work pending.

Under stream II of the SGRY twenty eight items of work were carried out in the year 2002-2003; 303 road works (WBM) were taken up and completed; 207 culverts were taken up, of which 196 have been successfully completed and the remaining 11 are in progress; the next priority was given to laying of threshing floors in the rural areas; 285 threshing floors were taken up and 263 have been successfully completed while the remaining 22 threshing floors are in progress; 123 works were taken up for repairing of the government hospital of which 116 have been completed while the remaining seven works are in progress except one item pending in laying of road work (cc) the rest, i.e., 70 works, have been carried out; 24 retaining walls were constructed and one is pending; the other works like bathing ghat, bus shelter, causeways, community centre, drainage, IMP to shandy, library building, oorani, other buildings, repairs to Panchayat office, shopping complex, supply channel, repairs to school building were also taken up and completed with just one or two items pending.

Targets and Achievements

Table 2.46 : Targets and Achievements of SGRY work in 2001-02 and 2002-03

Sl. No.	Name of the Scheme	Allotment (Rs. in lakhs)	No. of works taken up	No. of works completed	Expenditure
		2001-2002			
1.	Sampoorna Gramin Rozgar Yojana (Stream I)	485.55	518	518	485.55
2.	Sampoorna Gramin Rozgar Yojana (Stream II)	427.50	1090	1090	427.50
		2002-03			
1.	Sampoorna Gramin Rozgar Yojana (Stream I)	653.53	1216	1105	603.00
2.	Sampoorna Gramin Rozgar Yojana (Stream II)	645.03	1506	1495	605.03

Source: DRDA Records, Pudukkottai District.

Table 2.46 shows the financial targets and the physical achievements under the SGRY (Streams I & II) for the year 2001-02 and 2002-03. In the year 2001-02, under the SGRY stream I, 485.55 lakh rupees were allotted to carry out 518 works. By the end of the year all the 518 works were completed with the same cost value. In the same year, under the SGRY stream II, 1090 works were taken up at a target value of Rs.427.50 lakhs and all the works were completed with the same cost value by the end of the year. In the year 2002-03 1216 works were taken up, of which 1105 work were completed and 111 works are pending. Out of the allotted amount of Rs.653.53 lakhs, 603.53 lakh rupees has been spent by the administration. Under the second stream of the SGRY, 1506 works were taken up of the allotted amount of Rs.645.03 lakhs they have spent Rs.605.03 lakhs and completed 1495 works with 11 works pending.

Vayolagam Village Panchayat of Annavasal Union laid a threshing floor which is now in full use by the village people. The threshing floor constructed in the Panchayat is being utilized by the farmers for processing and drying their grains and pulses, such as beans, Bengal gram, black gram, green gram, horse gram, maize, millet, pea, red gram and paddy. The threshing floor was constructed with of stones for the floor with a slope to make it easy for tractors and other vehicles to enter and unload agricultural produce. While undertaking the construction work of the threshing floor the labourers were selected from the same Village Panchayat from the list of labourers/daily wage employees prepared by the Panchayat. The labourers were paid wages of Rs.54 per day. Of this 52 per cent was given as rice and the remaining 48 per cent was paid in cash to the labourers. The cost of the rice (5 kilogram @ Rs.5.65 per kilogram per day), i.e., Rs.28.25 was deducted and the remaining Rs.25.75 only was given to the labourers in cash. In Virachilai Panchayat of Thirumayam Block they laid a 68 meter cement concrete road at an estimated cost of Rs.54,825, of which Rs.32,695 was earmarked as labour component and Rs.21,930 was allotted for material component. This work was completed in twenty days with the utilization of fifty five labourers of that Village Panchayat. The wages comprised 52 per cent of rice and 48 per cent of cash. In order to carry out this task 55 labourers/ workers were selected from the daily wage employees list/ labourers list maintained in the Panchayat office.

Impact of the Scheme SGRY

Nowadays, due to water scarcity in the rural areas, agriculture is very poor and the people who are occupied in agriculture as a primary source of income are struggling for their livelihood. Because of the failure of monsoons, agricultural activities are severely affected and the agricultural labourers are not able to get adequate employment in the agricultural sector. In rural areas almost all the people depend on agriculture for their income. The agricultural coolies are also not able to get adequate employment to meet their daily requirements. Most areas of Tamil Nadu are severely affected by drought. The Government has taken several steps to provide relief from the drought like distributing thousands and thousands tonnes of rice to the drought affected areas free of cost. Under this scheme, by taking up works in the Panchayat area, an employment, i.e., additional wage employment is created in the rural areas. This is another form of creating employment for the daily wage employees. The concept of providing rice (5 kg @ 5.65 rupees) is now popular among the rural people. Compared to the rationshop rice, the price of this rice is less. So the people favour it. Moreover, some major works carried out under the SGRY scheme provide enduring benefits to the rural people. The works like tank desilting, road work, repairs to schools and hospitals, maintenance of oorani, threshing floor, shopping complex, bus shelter, causeways and SHG buildings are very useful to the rural people for their daily use.

The SGRY, through various works in rural areas, generates income to the people and provides wage employment to them. They are paid Rs.54 per day as wages for their work and this comprises rice, accounting for 52 per cent of the wages, and 48 per cent cash. After calculating the number of mandays and the employees employed, the wages are paid to the workers. Another important feature of this scheme is the ban on contractors. No middleman or any other intermediate agency should be employed for executing the works under this scheme. The full benefit of the wages to be paid should reach the villagers and the cost of the works should not involve any commission charges payable to contractors, middlemen or intermediate agencies. Muster rolls shall be maintained for every work separately showing the details of the wages paid to the workers and the foodgrains distributed.

DISTRICT SUPPLY AND MARKETING SOCIETY (DSMS)

About the Society

The District Supply and Marketing Society (DSMS) was started on 15-07-1994 in Pudukkottai District. The registered office of the society is located in the campus of the District Rural Development Agency (DRDA), Pudukkottai. Financial assistance of Rs.2.50 lakhs is being given by the DRDA, Pudukkottai, and initially UNICEF, Chennai, extended financial assistance of Rs.2.50 lakhs to the DSMS as one-time establishment expenditure. The society helps to implement the poverty alleviation programme continuously in pursuit of economic betterment of the poor womenfolk of the rural areas. The main objective of the society is to provide income generation and employment opportunities for the deprived class of womenfolk who virtually battle against poverty perpetually. The Swarnajayanthi Gram Swarozgar Yojana (SGSY) is a vital scheme implemented by the Ministry of Rural Development for the economic upliftment of women in the rural areas. This is a scheme designed to deliver socio-economic benefits directly to the deprived section of women in rural areas. Now there are 4,532 self help groups (SHGs) with a total membership of 74,795 (as on 24-04-2003) in Pudukkottai District. As per the governing body of the DSMS chaired by the District Collector, all the SHGs are to be registered with the DSMS with an annual subscription of Rs.100 per group.

Objectives

The District Supply and Marketing Society was established with the following objectives:

(1) To provide for and promote comprehensive marketing support to the SHGs in Pudukkottai District and to deal with relevant fields and factors contributing to the improvement of economic

development and social well-being of the SHG members. The groups may belong to trades like gem, quarry, pith, terracotta, korai mats, Tanjore art plates and new and different trades may also be included.

(2) To undertake activities like market identification and information, costing and price fixation, standardization and quality control, product design and packaging, transportation and storage, selling channels, advertising and promotion.

(3) To undertake and assist the organization of training and skill improvement courses, workshops, seminars etc.

(4) To aid, promote and coordinate research on its own or through other agencies including voluntary organizations (NGOs) and training centres to be established by the Government of Tamil Nadu.

(5) To analyse and propose solutions for specific problems encountered in the planning and implementation of various activities pursued by the several SHG groups.

(6) To prepare, print and publish brochures and other publicity materials in furtherance of the objectives of the society.

(7) To establish and maintain information services and to collaborate with other institutions, associations and societies in India or abroad interested in similar objectives.

(8) To do all such other lawful things as are conducive or necessary to the attainment of the above objectives or promote all round development of all the self help group families.

Programme and Activities

In order to realize the above objectives the society can either undertake directly or cause to be undertaken through other agencies the programmes listed hereunder:

(1) Marketing :

(i) Securing bulk orders from final buyers whether private or government.

(ii) Ensuring quality control and price fixation.
(iii) Arranging transportation of the produced materials.
(iv) Following up payments.
(v) Providing a common facility centre for the purpose of assisting SHGs and their members for storing, transporting, packing, processing, grading, branding etc.
(vi) Arranging financial inputs for the activity oriented and needy groups as some of the SHGs are in need of economic assistance, but find no bank coming forward to give credit in time.

(2) Training of the members of the self help groups.
(3) Arranging institutional credit by helping in the preparation of project proposals, procurement of tools and improved equipment or undertaking development linked activities.
(4) Arranging for the provision of explosives by obtaining a licences for the same.
(5) Making available new improved techniques and technologies to the SHGs thereby enhancing their productivity and reducing the drudgery of work.
(6) Lobbying and liaisoning with the Government/official machinery so as to effect policy changes for the benefit of the SHG groups. Sensitizing the government to the issues, needs and priorities of the self help groups will be the principal activity of the society.
(7) Purchasing and supplying raw materials wherever necessary.

Governing Body

The day to day management of affairs of the society shall vest with the Executive Committee in accordance with the byelaws of the society and the policies approved by the Governing Council of which the members are:

1. District Collector : Chairperson
2. Project Officer, DRDA : Vice-Chairman
3. Manager-cum-Secretary, DSMS : Member Secretary
4. Accounts Officer, DRDA : Treasurer

5.	General Manager, DIC	:	Member
6.	Assistant Project Officer (DWCRA) DRDA, Pudukkottai	:	Member
7.	Assistant Director (Mines)	:	Member
8.	Assistant Director of Khadi and Village Industries	:	Member
9.	Two representatives from quarry women	:	Member
10.	Two representatives for gem cutting women	:	Member
11.	Assistant General Manager (NABARD)	:	Member
12.	Two NGO representatives	:	Member
13.	Member of SHGs doing various economic activities	:	Member
14.	Lead Bank Manager	:	Member
15.	District Coordinator, Continuing Education Project	:	Member
16.	Assistant Manager, DSMS	:	Member
17.	Two scientists from among (a) STAMIN, Kudumiyanmalai (b) Veterinary University Research and Training Centre, Pudukkottai (c) Vamban Pulses Research Institute	:	Special Invitees

The tenure of the first Executive Committee shall be of 3 years. The control of the administration and the management of the affairs of the society shall vest with the Governing Council (GC) according to the rules and regulations of the society. The Governing Council will decide on the continuance or otherwise of any member or members of the Executive Committee depending on their utility and contribution. The basically required staff like manager-cum-secretary, accountant, marketing officer, sales assistant have been appointed and are at work. The society is functioning under the administrative control of the Department of Rural Development with the District Collector as its Chairman and the Project Officer, DRDA, as its Vice-Chairman.

Functioning

With financial assistance from DRDA, Pudukkottai, two four wheelers have been purchased, one under the IRDP infra (Jeep) and another under the SGSY (sales cum display van) for the sale of SGSY group products of the society. They are useful for selling SGSY group rural products at reasonable rates in trade fairs, shandies, weekly shandies and other places. Now the Pudukkottai District administration has taken up a new experiment to empower women quarry workers by vesting in them the lease rights of quarries and it has become a success story. A change in the living conditions of the quarry workers has been effected as a result of the direct ownership of the mining rights by the women self help groups under the SGSY scheme. Besides the improvement of their living standards, they have been set free from the clutches of the quarry contractors by the District Collector for 5 years and now 49 quarry women SHGs are functioning in Annavasal, Viralimalai, Kunnandarkoil, Thriumayam and Ponnamaravathy Panchayat Union areas. The Collector/Chairman, DRDA, has helped the quarry SHGs by issuing loans to these groups through the DSMS to remit the 1st instalment of the lease amount for the leased quarries.

For maintaining proper accounting of the group activities, Mahalir Thittam, the DSMS and the Arivoli Continuing Education are monitoring them effectively. Periodical meetings have been conducted by the District Collector and also by the Project Officer for reviewing the performance of the quarry groups. The District Collector has issued orders to all BDOs (VP) dated 12-03-2001 to purchase quarry materials produced by SHGs through the DSMS, Pudukkotai. So the quarry women are provided support in marketing their produce. The various government departments in the district have also been directed to purchase their requirements from the SHGs of the quarry women. They produce 60 mm and 49 mm metal and granite slabs. The DSMS has supplied materials not only to Pudukkottai District but also to the neighbouring district of Thiruvarur. The DSMS has also been supplying cut stone slabs to construct Women's Sanitary Complex in all Panchayats in Pudukkottai District. A tipper lorry was purchased by the DSMS costing Rs.8.00 lakhs under the provisions of the SGSY which helps transportation of the material. This tipper being run by the DSMS is now able to make a reasonable profit. Since the quarry leases were traditionally held by the local powerful people who also controlled the transportation and other infrastructure the tipper lorry comes handy in the movement of the product and reduces dependence. The lorry is made use of for other activities of the District Rural Development Agency when it is not used for quarry work, facilitating optimum use of the investment. So far more than Rs.11.06 lakh worth of materials have been transported by this tipper.

Two pumps with oil engines have been purchased to drain the quarry whenever it gets filled with water. Each of this cost Rs.29,000. They are now rented to the SHGs by the DSMS at reasonable rates. As the women work in the scorching sun, often with their children, small rest sheds have been constructed at the quarry sites where they can also eat their food. The women also get to take rest in these sheds. Thirteen sheds were built at a cost of Rs.20,000 each, totalling Rs.2.60 lakhs, under various schemes. Constant monitoring of the progress of the programme by the District Collector and the Project Officer, DRDA, and various line department officials ensures that the new social equations are not disturbed. This is significant as the traditional oppressive system tries to regain control. There have been instances were the NGO functionaries working among the quarry workers were intimidated in stray cases. The quarry worker women are also in the process of redefining themselves and are more confident now. Many of them also tried their hand at the recent local body elections. Major changes are happening in Annavasal, Viralimalai, Thirumayam and Ponnamaravathy Blocks, all in the relatively backward quarry areas of Pudukkottai District. Originally initiated by the then District Collector Srimathi.Sheela Rani Chunkath, I.A.S., the initiative has been sustained through time and in 2002 the Government of Tamil Nadu, based on the Pudukkottai experience, issued an order facilitating SHGs of BPL women to take leases of quarries at subsidized rates which is intended to benefit similar women in other districts as well.

The predominant rural industry in Pudukkottai District in respect of the old DWCRA groups is gem cutting. Twenty gem cutting machines have been purchased and rented out for the purpose of training-cum-production in S.Kulavaipatty of Thiruvarankulam Block. The rent is fixed at Rs.150 for each machine per month. During 1994 to 2002, the DSMS was engaged in the marketing of various rural products such as sambar powder, wire baskets, pith models, cut glass plates, paper machine dolls, greetings cards, Thanjavur picture paintings, glass blowing articles, terracotta, pottery, nylon mats, korai mats, pickles, cashewnuts, spices etc. and in supplying raw materials. In the above said period the DSMS had Rs.7.29 lakhs as sundry creditors and 4.72 lakhs as sundry debtors. In 2001-2002 the DSMS earned a net profit of Rs.2.90 lakhs. The sundry debtors amount is to be collected from various DWACRA group members and other institutions such as Poompuhar sales showrooms, Cauvery Supermarket etc.

The District Rural Development Agency, Pudukkottai, has released an amount of Rs.7.00 lakhs to start two sanitary marts in Pudukkottai District, one at Aranthangi and the other at Pudukkottai, for selling sanitary items like pans and p-traps, toilet cleaning brushes, toilet soaps etc. The DSMS is also engaged in the business of selling vegetables (like onion, cabbage, potato, tomato, carrot etc.) and operating a canteen at Uzhavarshandai, Pudukkottai. At present 113 self help groups are registered with the DSMS which supplies trade oriented raw materials like vine for (vine baskets), palm leaf, pith stick etc. to the groups. The activities of the DSMS are mainly service oriented, with a minimum amount (ranging from 10 per cent to 15 per cent) of profit for handicraft items. In the year 2001-2002, the DSMS sold handicraft items worth Rs.70,221 and quarry materials worth Rs.20,76,857. The DSMS is now attending to the needs and problems of the SHGs and DWACRA group members very effectively and with a sense of involvement. Hence the DSMS is indeed assisting and rendering service to the poor and struggling women in rural areas and making them free from the tentacles of poverty and unemployment. The DSMS is rendering services to the poor and needy women with the noble concepts of survival, development, respect, dignity, honour, justice and equality.

NON-CONVENTIONAL ENERGY INNOVATION

Biogas: An Eco-Friendly Energy

Biogas, where the required number of cattle are available, is an ideal fuel for rural households. It saves the scarce fuel wood reserves, very crucial in preventing deforestation in drought prone areas. It also helps the women who cook to have a smoke free kitchen, preventing many diseases. Since the slurry output of the biogas plant is a good manure it helps in generating more vegetation cover. For a water scarce and drought affected area like Pudukkottai District, biogas progress is of vital importance and the DRDA is giving priority to its promotion under the non-conventional energy programme of the government. However, the enthusiasm for biogas promotion was far from adequate in the district mainly due to the supplementary cost the beneficiary had to bear. To circumvent this hurdle in Pudukkottai District the DRDA adopted new strategies to help promote biogas.

To begin with the target area was reduced from the whole district to specific locations, the other areas to be covered in the following phase, keeping these as the nuclei. It was made sure that there was a functioning plant in the near vicinity of the selected locations. This was based on a participatory survey conducted of the number of cattle and the economic status of the families. The survey showed that the households, despite having cattle, had no pucca house, something peculiar about Pudukkottai District, perhaps due to the frequent droughts. It was decided to link the biogas programme with the housing scheme as a convergent programme. Two appropriate schemes, the Indira Awas Yojana (IAY) for upgradation of rural housing and the credit-cum-subsidy scheme were made use of in this effort. Those beneficiaries who needed upgradation of houses and had cattle were offered the biogas plant as well. Put together they now had the subsidy components of both the biogas and the housing scheme. The biogas programme now became attractive.

A massive awareness programme and a training programme

were conducted in Pudukkottai. Masonry training was imparted to a set of unemployed youth from the selected areas who now have a job and the units have experts' help available nearby. During the training programmes the masons' services were made available for construction of new plants. This has helped the beneficiaries to save on the cost as the construction charges are saved. The new approach has brought about dramatic changes in biogas implementation and more and more requests have begun to pour in, in contrast to the earlier situation. Thus while in 2001-20 80 units were built with difficulty, scattered all over the district in 42 locations, taking a period of 15 months, in 2002-03 105 plants were completed, centered round 7 habitations in four months' time. Out of the 105, 86 were tied up with housing programmes under both the IAY (upgradation) and the credit-cum-subsidy scheme (CCS). Many requests started coming in from the selected areas, where it became a need based programme.

As of now these are spread over Sempatoor Panchayat coming under Pudukkottai Panchayat Union, Melathoor Panchayat coming under Thiruvarankulam Block and Vallavari Panchayat in Aranthangi Block. Most of the plants are based on cow dung except a few which are based on human waste. The beneficiary families are fully dependent on biogas for cooking. Some of them are using biogas also for lighting, in some cases as an alternative during the frequent power failures in the area.

In an unusual case in a model plant at Melaputhuvayal the beneficiary is using the decade old KVIC drum model plant for running a deep well pumpset for domestic and irrigation purpose. This household has made substantial savings in fuel wood and diesel and uses the slurry as value added manure for a variety of crops. This beneficiary, Thiru.Thirunavukkarasu, a retired teacher of Melappathuvayal coming under Kunnandarkoil Block, has been using biogas for running the diesel pump for the past ten years. With minor modifications the pumpset was converted to use biogas. The engine is initially started on diesel, then the inlet of the biogas is turned on. With around 7 cattle, the Thirunavukkarasu family uses the biogas unit for both household uses and irrigation and the slurry formed is said to be an excellent manure. The slurry digested in anaerobic conditions, according to him, is also good as it saves the crops from weeds. Thirunavukkarasu, having enough cattle, has made substantial savings in this way as the use of diesel is the minimum and the annual savings works out to Rs.5000, without taking into account the savings on fuel wood. It is easy to operate and the need to run to diesel supply stations is also eliminated. People in the vicinity know about this successful unit and are eager to follow the retired teacher's path and many more farmers in surrounding villages now have biogas units. With frequent droughts biogas is an ideal energy for Pudukkottai region as this can save the scarce vegetation, routinely lost as fuel wood.

Innovations

— The earlier biogas promotion programme faced difficulties as the subsidy component was not attractive to the beneficiaries.

— It was decided to link the biogas programme to the IAY housing programme and the credit-cum-subsidy scheme (CCS).

— Those availing of the housing scheme were also provided with a biogas plant, the beneficiary getting the subsidy components of both.

— Beneficiaries themselves are provided training in operation and maintenance.

— Local unemployed youth are trained as masons.

— Geographical area is reduced to one location.

— Eventually it will spread out from such areas to the entire district.

3

AN INTERACTION WITH THE DISTRICT COLLECTOR

After conducting the field work and analyzing the process of implementation of all the schemes, the research team sought an appointment with the District Collector. He found an evening and allotted substantial time for discussion. A wide variety of questions were asked and to all the questions he responded readily. The responses are given hereunder.

The District Collector started working with people and their institutions, i.e., Panchayati Raj, as better results could be achieved and people could be satisfied. He moved in an unconventional way in implementing the schemes and programmes of the Central Government by giving the entire responsibility to the beneficiaries and the Panchayats. Of course now it has become a model and all district administrations have been instructed to follow the model of Pudukkottai. When the whole exercise was started, it was a calculated risk. He took the risk. When he was asked about his views on these experiments, he said that when he was an Additional Collector at Cuddalore, he witnessed the energy of the people in repairing the huts under the scheme of upgradation of katcha houses through a grant of Rs.10,000. People are not beneficiaries alone but development participants also. He explained further that when schemes are operated for the poor, the mindset of the poor has to be changed and their self respect and self esteem have to be protected and preserved. When we make the people owners they will take any initiate to achieve success. Otherwise they will continue to receive benefits but won't take any initiative. He tested his hypothesis in Cuddalore District where he was an Additional

Collector. His hunch was validated that ownership of the project determines the success of a project or a scheme. When decision making power is given to the people they take decisions. When they take decisions they are very cautious as they are responsible for any lapse. Even for minor repairs to their katcha house, they resort to several innovations. People not only have hands, legs and stomach, they also have ideas however illiterate they are. This kind of small changes in the district administration have created a very big change in the attitude of the people and the mindset of the beneficiaries. This change was reported in the Government of India, Rural Development Report 2001-2002. The Government can construct only houses but it cannot create a home. It could be done only by the people. If the responsibility of building houses is given to the beneficiaries they will make a home while building the house.

One cannot see life in the stereotyped houses. They are like mere hostels. Every one is unique in terms of physical and mental characters and features. According to the taste of each individual his house has to be constructed. No identical construction can be found in terms of designs and facilities when the owner of the house spends his money, for he takes care of everything. So far the free housing scheme of the Government has not created owners and, as a result, if there is any repair they seek the assistance of the Government as if the houses are owned by the Government. To change the mindset the District Collector contemplated a new idea. At the same time he wanted to undertake all innovations within the framework of the rules and regulations of the scheme. When it is done successfully in one place it can be replicated in all other places. It was his desire to make some changes in the methods and procedures that had been followed in the past for implementing programmes and schemes. It was full of risk but he took the risk. Till the completion of the work he did not inform anyone. Only after seeing the success he informed all. In implementing programmes and schemes an array of officials are involved. But when the whole responsibility is entrusted to the people the officials develop an apathy till they see the results.

Normally a myth is floated that when a work is given to

contractors, it will be done quickly and that they are always amenable and controllable. They will go by the direction of the officials. Sometimes they carry out works even on oral instructions. But people cannot be treated as contractors. They will take their own time. They cannot be controlled and they will not dance to the tune of the officials. When any work is given to the beneficiaries they will take their own time and there will be a delay in completing the work. This has been the view of the lower level officials also. When this was brought up for discussion with the Collector he responded to all the above propositions and arguments. He said that normally officials are interested in completing the work and achieving the target in time and getting the name without looking into the implications of the work. This has damaged all our development work. When it is given to the people they first make themselves owners of the programme or work. They look at the implications of the work. This process is more important than completing the work. IAY house construction was entrusted to the beneficiaries. They first started recognizing themselves as owners. Secondly it was a fulfillment of their dreams. For the officials it was only a building but to the beneficiary it was a home. He is going to live in it and hence he takes time to design and match the money to his requirements. With this perception the beneficiaries are given time for completing the work. To officials finishing the work is the be all and the end all. But one has to look at the process and from that perspective it is all the more important to make the beneficiaries the owners. When contractors delay the construction work we accept it and when the beneficiaries delay it for a week we raise a hue and cry. It is the mindset of the officials which has to be changed.

Yet another success he has achieved in implementing the programme through beneficiaries is transparency and efficiency. From the selection of beneficiaries to the completion of the work transparency is ensured since middlemen are kept out. The district administration provides the guidelines to the beneficiaries and training is also given to them. No one can cheat them because they are empowered.

Normally in the houses constructed by the Government for the poor smokeless chulas and toilets are only showpieces and are not being used. But in this case barring a few all are in use. This is because toilets have been constructed in the place suitable to the beneficiaries. Even then a few have not used them. So a new device is to be adopted from the next year: the last installment of Rs.2,000 will be released only after checking the use of toilets. When they start using the toilets it will become a culture by itself.

In the case of the Women's Sanitary Complex in the light of the experience gained consultations are now held with the user groups before constructing the building. The availability of water in the complexes is also ensured. The District Collector stated that from 2003-04 onwards the construction work will be given to the user groups. He said that it is necessary to make the people owners of the Government programmes and schemes making the officials only facilitators rather than providers. Though programmes are designed by the people through the Panchayats, now all the programmes are implemented by the Panchayats. Ultimately the people should own the programmes of the Government as the programmes of the people.

He has a strong belief that people, as long as they are a political, are sincere, honest and look at problems from the perspective of the community and follow ethical values. When they are driven by the political forces they are oriented to look at problems from the perspective of party politics. All good work will be appreciated by all. There is no barrier to initiating good work in any field. The District Collector impresses one by his openness, faith in people and transparency.

4

AN INTERACTION WITH THE PROJECT OFFICER, DRDA

As a result of the discussions with the development participants, local level officials and the District Collector, it was perceived that the role of the Project Office, DRDA, is crucial at the district level for the success of any scheme or programme and hence it was decided to have an interaction with the Project Officer, DRDA, of Pudukkottai District. Based on the decision, the research team had an interaction with Mr. Selvarajan, Project Officer, DRDA, on various issues relating to Panchayat Raj System and rural development activities.

He answered all the questions based on his experience. Generally it is perceived that officials construe the Panchayat as an unwanted phenomenon and people's representatives as having poor capacity to carry out activities as effectively and efficiently as officials. But Mr. Selvarajan was of the different view that Panchayats have tremendous potential and this potential has to be utilized by the officials for the successful implementation of schemes. He felt that Panchayats partners in the governance of development and in the administration of social justice. Panchayats bring transparency to the administration and this reduces corruption. Now people have come to the stage of asserting their rights and claiming their dues. At this stage the Panchayat institutions will reduce the burden of the officials and the State governments. For better functioning of Local Bodies both officials and the leaders have to be oriented, conscientised and trained in Panchayati Raj management and in administering development. By building the capacity and skill of the Panchayat leaders effective service delivery is ensured. The training can be continuous. Mr. Selvarajan said that there are inbuilt weaknesses in the system which can be corrected only by the State government.

While asking about the role of the government, he replied that the government, through its bureaucracy, facilitates the activities of the Panchayats. It is the duty of the Panchayat Presidents to mobilize the people for development activities and they are to be used by the government departments while carrying out their sectoral department programmes. People should be prioritized. Mr. Selvarajan felt that supply driven activities are still going on. Yet, at the district level, there are possibilities of synergizing various departments to deliver effective services with the involvement of the Panchayats and the coordination of the District Collector. In Pudukkottai, the District Collector, by his sincerity and commitment, took up several programmes with the involvement of the beneficiaries and the Panchayats. He provided the necessary leadership and the Project Officer enabled both the beneficiaries and the Panchayats to carry out the government programmes and schemes to the satisfaction of the community.

There is yet another question which is quite important and serious, namely, the convergence of department or synergization of departments for a common cause. In India it is very difficult to bring about convergence among departments. Panchayats also face the same problem. No line department cooperates with the Panchayats. They act independently and they never bother to get the opinion of the people through the Panchayats. Mr. Selvarajan was asked to react to this. He said that it is true, but added that if the District Collector is an able leader, he will be able to stop this. The District Collector looks after not only law and order but also all development activities. Through close interaction and monitoring the District Collector can make various departments synergize for a specific work. He cited many examples from Pudukkottai District, whereby Pudukkottai District stands first in rural development activities.

There is yet another major area which hinders the process and speed of development, namely, strict observance of rules and regulations. Rural development schemes are implemented throughout the country and the state. In a vast country local conditions vary from one place to another, one district to another, one state to another. How can the rules and procedures can be followed very strictly in all the areas?

He said that all the rural development schemes have a great deal of flexibility and scope for innovation. How the scope and flexibility are utilized by the district administration matters much. In Pudukkottai District, the District Collector passes orders with all details in the best interests of the people. No administration will find fault with such flexible operations. Rural development programmes have a flexibility, which is being judiciously used by the District Collector.

There is a much debated issue at all levels, namely, the commitment of the officials and their capability. Mr. Selvarajan openly admitted that the officials' capacity has to be enhanced. There are officials who have commitment and capabilities and do produce results. But many lack vision, vigour, commitment, enthusiasm but even they can be transformed in due course as people exert pressure on them.

He further said that he has been learning everyday from the field. People have enormous common sense. They act on their common sense. They have not only problems. They have solutions also. On many occasions officials fail to understand the perception and attitude of the people.

Corruption was another topic of the interview. He specifically talked about administrative corruption. He said that corruption can be defined in many ways. Corruption refers to unethical way of taking public money for the private purse. There are inbuilt weaknesses in the system. If money is taken from one head to another head for public activity which is essential, from the auditor's point of view it is not correct. The system has to be oriented to the reality. Till then this kind of transaction will continue in administration. One has to see that no one in the administration takes public money for his private use. He suggested that social audit should be established for all the departments.

For the effective functioning of the district administration he pinned his hope on the District Collector's stern effort in all activities.

The District Collector is considered to be the role model and the attitude of the District Collector orients and motivates all the officials working under him to make the district a role model for other districts. The District Collector metes out proper treatment to all spheres of activities and his leadership did not had any vested interest. His activities are transparent and visible and his open mindedness paves the way for the successful district administration. His recognition of and appreciation for good work motivates the officials of the district to work better.

When he was asked about the political intervention while doing his work he said that he will follow the path of practical uprightness. He will make himself clear to the others about his way of functioning and he will not compromise while going strictly by the rules which are meant for the poor and other vulnerable sections of the society.

Finally, he attributed the successful functioning of the DRDA to the convergence of various departments in implementing the schemes. Sustainable development can be made possible through the like mindedness and open mindedness of officials in carrying out the activities. He too has the idea that development is not possible through coercion and that it will be make possible only through goodwill gestures. Apart from this he stated the following reasons for the successful implementation of schemes:

1. He doesn't have the feeling of being an officer but considers himself one among the people.
2. He considers his job as an opportunity to serve the people.
3. He learns many things from models at the grassroots.
4. Convergence and clubbing of various schemes into the priorities of the people is one of the secrets of his success.
5. Learning from the field which provides enough opportunity for success.
6. His success is due to the risk taken by him under the guidance of the District Collector.
7. Ultimately the guidelines themselves provide a lot of scope for better functioning if interpreted properly and considered an indicative list.

INTEGRATED ANALYSIS

To obtain maximum benefits from each programme various innovations are being tried. The attempts made by the district administration of Pudukkottai in this direction are analysed hereunder.

Government Guidelines

Conforming to the government guidelines, but exploiting the flexibility provisions, the DRDA, Pudukkottai, incorporated various innovations while implementing schemes. In the Indira Awas Yojana they tried innovations in design, building materials, construction and labour use. Following this the beneficiaries opted for staircases, designs meant to accommodate animals also etc. The device of forming user groups has become a successful venture in the case of the Women's Sanitary Complex. It is an interesting development and the steps taken in the district were appreciated by the Directorate of Rural Development of Tamil Nadu, which advised the other districts to follow the same pattern. When steady progress has been made in the routine programmes again innovations are being tried. Thus in Pudukkottai District the construction of multipurpose centres for the SHGs, normally constructed through contractors, has been entrusted to the self help group members themselves. Taken up under the food for work programme, the Sampoorna Grameen Rozgar Yojana (SGRY), this has led to a situation wherein the rice being made available is actually reaching the poor without the hindrances normally encountered. The availability of low cost rice in plenty takes care of the food requirements of the people. To augment and restore the traditional drinking water support systems in the region, drinking water ponds called ooranis have been taken up under various programmes. In all more than 130 ooranis have been taken up, mainly under the SGRY and the 11th Finance Commission grants at a cost of Rs.210 lakhs. Empowering women receives major attention under the various programmes. In this endeavour the role of the fully functional District Supply and Marketing Society (DSMS) in Pudukkottai District is worth mentioning. Originally set up under the IRDP programme, the DSMS is doing yeomen service in alleviating indebtedness among rural women. Intended to provide support in promoting rural industries and marketing rural products, the Pudukkottai DSMS plays a major role in empowering the quarry worker SHGs by providing credit and marketing support. In an experiment to see if the DSMS can play a role in accessing credit from banks, which are normally hesitant in advancing loans to BPL populations without adequate guarantees, the DSMS has now successfully availed of a loan of Rs.15 lakhs from the Indian Overseas Bank, which in turn it lends to the SHGs. For a water scarce and drought affected area like Pudukkottai District the biogas programme is of vital importance and the DRDA is giving priority to its promotion under the non-conventional energy programme. The enthusiasm for biogas promotion was far from adequate in the district originally mainly due to the supplementary cost the beneficiary had to bear. To circumvent this hurdle the DRDA adopted new strategies to help promote biogas. The target area was reduced to a specific location, other areas to be covered in the following phases. It was also decided to link the biogas programme to the housing scheme as a convergent programme. Two appropriate schemes, the Indira Awas Yojana for upgradation of rural housing and the credit-cum-subsidy scheme were made use of in this. Those beneficiaries who needed upgradation of their rural house and had cattle were offered the biogas plant as well. Put together they now had the subsidy components of both the biogas and the housing scheme. This was made possible only because of the flexibility provisions in the government guidelines governing these schemes.

Training and Transparency

Training officers and staff, Panchayati Raj Institutions, self help group members and NGOs have been given top priority in Pudukkottai District and the SGSY programme in particular has received a major thrust in the process. Of particular importance is the increased involvement of the Block Development Officers and the supporting staff in promoting the self help group concept and following up the process. The training imparted in project preparation has helped in conceptualization of numerous income generating activities. Constant monitoring by the District Collector and the Project Officer, DRDA, also ensures transparency and accountability. This training input is to be a long term investment in the development potential of the district.

Circulation of pamphlets in Tamil on various schemes to the users and the field staff, publication of the monthly newsletter "Pudugai Punal" for the benefit all SHGs and Village Panchayats and selected NGOs are among the activities in this direction. The District Collector also sends relevant materials on specific themes to the Gram Sabha which gets circulated to PRIs and SHG members. This has made the implementing team more confident.

The Thiruvarankulam Block of Pudukkottai District taken a step ahead and displayed a board in front of the office giving the details of the work available under the SGRY programme. The board presents the total work available, total number of mandays required and the number of labourers required for completing the work. Those who are interested can register their name with the respective Panchayats. Through this type of activity transparency is maintained and the role of intermediatories and exploiters is nullified.

Level of Participation

Participation is the key component in development discourse. Participation in governance pertains to the process by which citizens, particularly poor and marginalized ones, influence and take control of the resources and decisions that directly affect them. The right to participate in governance is seen as a right rather than a favour bestowed by the government. This right allows citizens to claim other rights and entitlements. In this sense, citizen participation becomes more than a technical fix. It is a good thing not simply because it makes government programmes and services more effective and sustainable but because it creates a dynamics wherein people can engage the government for the benefit of the larger population that is often excluded from formal political affairs. Suiting the above mentioned points the innovations made in the implementation ensure people's participation at all levels of the schemes. The role of the government stops with the selection of beneficiaries. Even in that process, Panchayati Raj Institutions play a significant role. PRIs are called decentralized governing institutions in which people's participation at a high level is ensured. In the case of the IAY the responsibility rests with the beneficiary from getting the work order to the completion of the house. In the Women's Sanitary Complex collective participation is ensured from the maintenance of the asset to running it like a business enterprise. The food for work programme satisfies the needs of the unemployed and also provides food for those who participate in schemes on non-wage days. The DSMS supports the rural women and enhances their participation in income generation activities. The biogas facility makes the beneficiaries participate in the ongoing movement on ecology and resource conservation.

Project Ownership

Once it was held that development agencies and governments knew all the problems of the citizens, had all the necessary answers and therefore implemented all the right programmes. Citizens were merely beneficiaries of the fruits of expert thinking and know-how that guided development initiatives. In the 1980s the failure of many of these "blueprint approaches" pointed to the critical role of the ordinary citizens in ensuring the success of development initiatives. So, citizens began to be invited to participate in and to incorporate their needs into projects to make sure that these were acceptable and appropriate to their "counterpart contributions"--mostly in the form of voluntary labour. These were also considered important in that these reduced the cost of development. The issue of "project ownership" thus gained significance. For projects to work, the "community"--perceived as a homogenous social group that had shared interests--had to have a sense of ownership of the programmes to pursue and achieve the desired results. More and more communities were drawn into the entire project cycle of identification, planning, implementation, monitoring and evaluation of impact. Thus, the poor began to be recognized as "choosers" and "users" of development. At about this time, there was much rethinking about the role of the state and the government in economic development. There was a growing belief that the state had to be "rolled back" so that the market mechanism could do its job of promoting economic growth. Community development thus progressed into the mode of promoting self-reliant development. The poor were seen no longer as "beneficiaries" but as "consumers" who could "buy into" development initiatives. This was proved in Pudukkottai District and the results are in amply visible in terms of innovations.

Socio-Economic Impact

In Pudukkottai District a unique experiment is underway wherein women quarry workers, who were living in conditions of bonded labour under quarry contractors, have been organized under SHGs and quarry leases awarded to them. This has led to major changes in the social scene in the backward regions of the district. The women quarry workers in Pudukkottai District have been given lease rights and the initial lease amount given as a loan, easily repayable in instalments, by the DRDA through the DSMS. The DSMS set up under the DRDA mainly for marketing rural products, has played a key role as have the local NGOs. This programme has benefited an estimated 540 families from below poverty line sections to come out of their BPL status. This has liberated many women from BPL families from indebtedness as the difference in interest rates when borrowing from moneylenders is as much as 40 to 50 per cent. In general, with the active support of the DSMS, which works in close cooperation with NGOs, women of the district have gained in confidence and they are now in leadership positions. The house design chosen by the beneficiary himself makes him feel proud that he has attained a social status on par with other elevated classes in society. This kind of social and economic impact was created because of the innovations tried by the district administration in implementing government schemes. They have linked various programmes so that the beneficiary may avail of the combined facilities. One example to note here is that the SGSY programme demands that a group has to reach certain stages in order to avail of credit. But where the women coming for loans are already engaged in viable economic activities and intended to do it in groups the DSMS comes forward to give loans. Eventually they get transformed into the routine SGSY groups. Even where they are organized as per SGSY guidelines there are cases where bank loans are delayed or are not forthcoming at all despite all efforts. Here again the DSMS loans come handy.

Empowering and Enabling Women

Empowering women receives major attention in the various programmes. Following this path the DSMS is doing service to the womenfolk in alleviating their indebtedness. So far 43 groups have availed of the facility of lending through the DSMS. This has liberated many women from BPL families from indebtedness as the difference in interest rates when borrowing from moneylenders is as much as 40 to 50 per cent. In general, with the active support of the DSMS which works in close cooperation with NGOs, women of the district have gained in confidence and they are now in leadership positions. In the case of the quarry worker women there is a major change as they were once in near bonded labour conditions. Further, the hundred member strong user group of the Women's Sanitary Complex, with their frequent meetings and lending capacity, has also become a power centre in the respective villages and the women members are now significant players in rural society. They have also become more confident as they are playing a major role in community resource management, some of them becoming natural leaders in the process. Women have also been trained in technology, including masonry, for long term sustainability. Self help groups of rural women are now building their own houses. The Pudukkottai District administration has taken the following steps to empower and enable women:

-- Enhancing women's access to and control over productive endowments.
-- Increasing the productivity of women's labour by expanding their access to extension services, credit, education, information and training and influencing the process of knowledge creation.
-- Increasing women's returns on their labour and produce by expanding their access to commodity and labour markets and their ability to affectively bargain in the market place.

Accountability and Responsiveness

There will never be enough resources in the public sphere. So it becomes all the more important that the government should effectively manage the available the resources in the best possible way. This means that public resources have to be managed to respond to citizens' priority needs. Directly connecting with citizens will allow this to happen in a manner that can meaningfully draw from both local knowledge and experience in an inclusive and participatory way. Governments and public officials need to be accountable and transparent to citizens about their actions, particularly in relation to their public service mandates and the use of public resources. This will create a situation wherein the citizen and the government can go hand in hand to achieve their target. This too was also followed in Pudukkottai District. The use of the Women's Sanitary Complex is one of the fine examples of the above.

Implementation of schemes at the district level involves greater responsibility for putting the selected strategies into action. The district administration requires the support of not only the state, the local political elites and the bureaucracy but also the people's active involvement and genuine participation at all levels in both selection and implementation of schemes. The process evolved out of the experiment by the Pudukkottai District administration proves its credibility and obviously ensures people's participation.

Social Equality

Delivery of goods and services to the target groups, particularly to the weaker sections in rural areas, should result in social equality. About 80 per cent of the beneficiaries of the IAY scheme are socially underprivileged sections of the society who now possess a decent house to live in. Through this they feel that they have attained a higher social status than before. The user group of the Women's Sanitary Complex has 100 members from all sections of the society and an opportunity has been provided to all to become stakeholders in public property. In some Women's Sanitary Complexes the role of the caretaker is under circulation every month, giving equal chance to all the members. Similarly, the DSMS not only strives to improve the economic condition of rural womenfolk but also, through their economic activities, makes them attain social equality with the women of other strata in the society.

Environmental Conservation

Keeping in mind the sustainability of the resources, development approaches are now designed to save the resources for future generations also. The mud block technology introduced by the DRDA proves this. This technology serves two purposes. One is moulding durable blocks without over exploiting the natural resources and the other one is the simultaneous process of tank desiltation. Planting of trees before IAY houses and garden maintenance behind the Women's Sanitary Complex using the wastewater help to

conserve the environment to some extent. The thrust on the use of non-conventional energy resources, especially biogas, helps to save the environment from smoke and emission of carbon di-oxide while consumption non-renewable of fuel woods and liquid fuels is also minimized. Therefore these attempts in Pudukkottai District are in line with the process of environmental conservation.
Finally, the innovative practices adopted by Pudukkottai District are presented in a nutshell hereunder.

(1) Involvement of beneficiaries in the construction of IAY houses, choosing their own design type besides contributing their labour and opting for cost effective technology.
(2) Building the concept of "collective ownership" and formation of "user group" in order to maintain public property effectively was achieved through the Women's Sanitary Complex.
(3) Giving employment opportunity and food to rural folk while ensuring maintenance of infrastructure facility was achieved with the help of the food for work programme.
(4) Linking of various schemes while availing of the basic facilities of all of them was achieved in Pudukkottai District through the provision of biogas plants linked to upgradation of houses.
(5) The activities of the DSMS are commendable. Only a few districts have set up the District Supply and Marketing Society and the Pudukkottai District experience has proved its value.
(6) Apart from all these, the Pudukkottai District experiment in innovations serves as a pioneering model for the other districts in Tamil Nadu.

We are living in a time of transition. For some observers, the human race is entering its "global age"; it is a precious, often undemocratic journey which cannot be shunned, but must be navigated with trepidation and care. The globalization of markets and money, politics and people is imbued with fearsome ambiguity. It is a period in which the nation state may be in terminal decline, yet there is a simultaneous rebirth of atavistic, often bloody nationalism. Analyzing the thesis and antithesis of global integration versus national sovereignty is the praxis of the age. The nature of governmental institutions, the functions they carry out and the manner in which these roles are performed, have been subjected to an unprecedented series of changes throughout the world since the early 1980s. The dynamics of this change has come from:

- Technical innovations,
- An attempt at paradigmatic redefinition of the role of the state and state organizations.

In this context the New Public Management is increasingly utilized to explain the attempt to redefine administrative culture and structures. These attempts at a cultural reform are a collection of global mega trends which are:

- Attempts of many governments to check the growth of government.
- The internationalization of public administration.
- Automation in public administration.

The rise of the NPM (New Public Management) has proved seemingly inexorable, although attempts to check the growth of government, privatization, automation and indeed the internationalization of public administration may be all seen to be adjuncts to or elements of the New Public Management.

The initiative taken by the Pudukkottai District administration in terms of the New Public Management strategy resulted in an astounding outcome with quality service. The attitudinal change of the government in making the beneficiary a development participant is considered an enormous success. Making the people participate in the development process is a long cherished dream of the development analyst and the innovations attempted by the Pudukkottai District administration have transformed the concept of "citizen participation" into a reality. Further, on the part of the government, some significant changes in the service mode can be easily identified. Quality service is now provided instead of concentrating on quantity of service, which is merely statistics with no stress on utility, endurance and acceptance of the scheme. In the case of the IAY houses handing over the task of house construction to the beneficiary effected a drastic change in the quality of the houses as compared to earlier group houses and hence the result was obvious. The introduction of the Women's Sanitary Complex created a rewarding situation for rural womenfolk and also served the purpose of total rural sanitation.

Similarly the food for work scheme of the SGRY came to the rescue of the poverty stricken rural masses in addition to effecting renovation and infrastructure building in rural India. The DSMS lends support to the upcoming women entrepreneurs of SHGs which will empower them socially and economically. All these actions aimed at quality service supplement the process of development in rural India which is being attempted for more than five decades.

Another phenomenon to be mentioned is the value perception of the government and the beneficiaries about the schemes. To shrink the role of the government is the need of the hour. It may be forced by internal and external forces to deliver quality services. The government must assume the role of facilitator in all its actions and change from the development process to the business mode. The beneficiaries' expectations are high. Rather than the money they want to fulfil their expectations. So nowadays they have started involving themselves in all activities to get their demands. They value each and every opportunity not only for economic upliftment but also to attain a social status. This can be seen clearly from the views expressed by the IAY beneficiaries. The Pudukkottai District administration deserves appreciation for its innovation and painstaking effort to implement the schemes effectively. The insight into the new plan was streamlined by the officials and the whole task could not have been achieved without the efforts and the cooperation of the officials. The autonomy given to the officials to operate the schemes was an added advantage. Now the bureaucratic state takes a new incarnation as an effective, efficient and credible bureaucracy which functions on the basis of results and not on hard and fast rules. Activities are driven by goals and not by rules. The focus is not on inputs but on the outcome. The outcome is not measured quantitatively as done earlier but on the basis of the impact created by the scheme and its implementation. The open minded attitude of the government officials made these things possible. Further the proper use of available human and technological resources contributed to the great success of these schemes. Human resources were utilized well in the IAY, the SGRY and the Women's Sanitary Complex schemes in a productive and constructive manner. India being the most populous country in the world, these kinds of initiatives will be doubly fruitful. Introduction of indigenous technologies will further ease the implementing process with an eco-friendly mechanism.

6

OBSERVATIONS AND CONCLUSION

While looking at the implementation of programmes like the IAY, the WSC, food for work, DSMS and biogas, the following were obvious:

(1) Government, based on the need of the hour, has modified its rules and regulations. The concept of citizen friendly and citizen caring administration has come into existence.

(2) The measures taken by the district administration to ensure participation of the beneficiaries in the implementation of the programmes have been fruitful.

(3) Transparency in the functioning of the administration has also helped in bringing about the desired results.

(4) The effort taken by the district administration to reconcile the interest of the citizen with that of the role of the state is a remarkable change in the role of the government.

(5) The present process attempts to articulate the connection between the economic dependence of vulnerable groups in the ongoing process and the role of the state in facilitating the upliftment of the rural masses from their obscurity.

(6) The innovative practices adopted by the district administration emphasized targets and stressed the role of government as mission driven with a flavour for enterprise.

(7) Reduction of bureaucratic rules ultimately led to the success of these programmes.

(8) The development of a result oriented system is a boon to Indian democracy.

Implementation of schemes through people's participation and innovative methods carried out by the Pudukkottai District administration show that rural development is no longer a distant dream. Beneficiaries, as development participants also contribute to the success of the programmes framed for their upliftment. Attitudinal changes on the part of both the administration and the beneficiaries, leading to efficiency and effectiveness in administration, has become a significant factor in the administrative history of India. The measures taken by the Pudukkottai District administration in all forms from bringing about transparency in administration to creating a positive impact on the beneficiaries' life socially and economically has paved way for the success. The efforts taken by the officials in providing training and guidance to the beneficiaries were much greater than in the earlier experiment. In the case of the government's rural housing scheme earlier houses were built and handed over to the people but now the beneficiaries are constructing their own houses with the government's help. These kinds of procedural changes with innovative techniques will in the long run, give positive outcomes. Further, painstaking efforts on the beneficiary's part in terms of severe hardwork and group task have made them the owners of the project. Collective ownership is once again rejuvenated in the Women's Sanitary Complex. The concept of user group inculcates responsibility in the users to maintain their asset. Through this experiment two kinds of goals are achieved: on the one hand the government has provided a welfare measures to the people and on the other the people have to safeguard their property given by the government. This will ensure the success and sustainability of any scheme. The enthusiasm shown by the stakeholders and the efforts taken by the district administration have gone hand in hand ultimately leading to the New Public Management. Through this experiment transparency, high level of peoples' participation, sense of ownership, empowering and enabling of women, greater accountability and responsibility with social equity and environmental conservation have been ensured.

The administration, hitherto tainted by red tapism and delay, incompetence and corruption has started rethinking its role. Negative cannotations of the bureaucracy and the ever-expanding nature of the bureaucracy have given way to thoughts of discipline, precision and reliability. The bureaucratic work force has now adopted procedural and structural changes in their mechanism to ensure people's participation, transparency, accountability and also to ensure positive outcome from their actions. The Pudukkottai experiment has amply prove the changes overtaking in the administration and the innovations carried out show that the administration has made the people participants from mere spectators of the ongoing development process in the country. Lubricants in the form of flexible rules and regulations reduce the friction in the administration, which results in efficiency, effectiveness and economy. The administrative system, in modern parlance, should restructure itself to fulfil the citizen's aspirations. Laudable development programmes, plans and projects can not be successful unless a "people-centered" governing mechanism is operationalized. Rule oriented administration, in the course of five decades, has only proved its inefficiency and the government has learnt a good lesson. Now the government is oriented towards the task for better results.

Another important aspect to be noted in the change in the administrative system is that it is geared towards meeting human needs. People, who were regarded as beneficiaries so far have become "development participants" so that they can identify the priorities of their needs and prepare a plan of action by themselves to suit their demands. The government can shrink its role to be a facilitator by providing them with what they need and assisting them when required. Classical theorists have their faith in the administrative structure and procedure and hope that it will bring prosperity to the country. But contemporary experiments have proved that having faith in the people rather than in the administrative structure and procedure will lead to good results. This alternative to development also cares for the future generation, ensuring sustainable development and greater concern for the environment. The development process and environmental degradation run parallel to each other ultimately endangering our future. Hence, development activities should focus their attention on environmental protection also. The initiatives taken by the Pudukkottai District administration by merging the environmental protection programme with developmental activities has added another feather to its cap. The cry of the earth to save the younger generation was taken into account. Even though their achievement was small it may grow larger in the future. More fuel consumption is not only over exploits the inner core of the earth and deforestation depletes the ozone layer. The minor efforts taken by the Pudukkottai District administration to propagate the idea of biogas for household purposes will give a major thrust to environmental protection. Similarly the introduction of mud block technology for construction purposes is also a major effort to protect the environment. These were made possible only because of the people's participation. People's participation is regarded as another way to accelerate the process of development coupling the people with the administration. Transparency can be ensured by people's participation because it will mitigate the bureaucratic evils of rigidity, insensitivity, unresponsiveness and red-tapism and eradicate intermediaries. This strategy of the New Public Management has created the space for an accountable and a responsible administration by introducing innovations and transparency. It has also taught the administrator to cultivate the quality of a broad outlook on public affairs so that he can help the public rather than get bogged down in rigid rules and regulations.

The New Public Management therefore has brought about a great change in three dimensions. The first dimension relates to the scope of the administration, reducing its role to that of a facilitator from that of a provider; the second dimension relates to the perspective of the administrator, changing his mindset from that of a bureaucrat to that of a public servant; and the third dimension relates to the people seeing them as development participants and not as beneficiaries. These changes in the administration will lead to a sunlit path in the process of the development of third world countries.

BIBLIOGRAPHY

Allen Shick, "Towards the Cybernetic State", *Transaction,* Vol.7, Feb.1970.

Ali Sofi, and Anita Rao; "Reinventing Public Administration for 21st Century, *Indian Journal of Public Administration*, Vol. XLVI, No.2, April-June, 2000.

Asmerom, K.H., K.Borgman and R.Hoppe, "Good Governance, Decentralization and Democratisation in Post-Colonial State", *Indian Journal of Public Administration*, Vol.41, No.4, Oct-Dec, 1985.

Box, Richard C., Gary S.Marshall, B.J.Reed, "New Public Management and Substantive Democracy", *Public Administration Review*, Vol. 61, 2001.

Christopher Pollitt, Geert Bouckaert, *Public Management Reform: A Comparative Analysis*, Oxford; Oxford University Press, 1999.

Divedi, O.P. and K.M.Henderson, "Development Alternatives: Alternative Administration", *Indian Journal of Public Administration*, Vol.XLII, No.I, January-March, 1996.

Ewan Ferlic, *The New Public Management in Action*, Oxford: Oxford University, 1996.

George, H. Frederickson, *New Public Administration*, Alabama: University of Alabama, 1980.

Jan-Erik Lane, *The Public Sector: Concept, Models and Approaches*, New Delhi: Sage Publications, 1995.

Jaspal Sing, "Effectiveness of Bureaucracy", *Indian Journal of Public Administration*, Vol. XLVI, No.2, April-June, 2000.

Jerry, Larry D., "From Greek Mythology to the Real World of New Public Management and Democratic Governance", *Public Administration Review*, Vol. 59, 1999.

Minocha, O.P., "Good Governance: New Public Management Perspective" in Chadurvedi (ed), *Towards Good Governance*, New Delhi: IIPA, 1999.

Moe, Ronald C., "The 'reinventing government' exercise: Misinterpreting the problem, misjudging the consequences", *Public Administration Review*, Vol. 54, 1994.

Moore, Mark.H., *Creating Public Value: Strategic Management in Government*, Harvard: Harvard University, 1995.

Moore, Mick, "Declining to learn from the East: The World Bank on Governance and Development", *IDS Bulletin*, Vol.24, No.6, 1993.

Murthy, Ranjani (ed), *Building Women's Capacities: Interventions in Gender Transformation*, New Delhi: Sage Publications, 2001.

INDEX